LORING AIR FORCE BASE THROUGH TIME

JOSEPH T. PAGE II

AMERICA THROUGH TIME®
ADDING COLOR TO AMERICAN HISTORY

This book is dedicated to the men and women of Loring Air Force Base

Fonthill Media Inc.
www.fonthillmedia.com
office@fonthillmedia.com

First published 2023

ISBN 978-1-63499-494-1

Typeset in Mrs Eaves XL Serif Narrow
Printed and bound in England

CONTENTS

ACKNOWLEDGMENTS

Foremost, I would like to thank my parents: Joseph and Kathleen. Here is another one for your book collection!

Immense thanks to Mr. Kevin Rutherford for involving me in recording the rich history of Loring. Kevin and I virtually "met" through updating Wikipedia pages relating to the histories of United States Air Force (USAF) bases around the world. While some of our edits may have clashed (at first), we reached a mutual understanding and respect for the material being created and updated.

Eternal gratitude for Alan Sutton, president of Fonthill Media. Alan took a chance on this project to build Fonthill's backlist, so I hope it represents a positive example of an enjoyable pictorial history.

Additional thanks to all Loring AFB veterans and their stories of living in the northeastern part of the United States. Their sacrifice has not gone unnoticed.

Finally, I would like to thank my wife and children for their patience with my writing endeavors.

All photos, except where noted, were sourced from the Air Force Historical Research Center at Maxwell Air Force Base, Alabama.

Introduction

Loring Air Force Base (AFB) was the first postwar United States Air Force (USAF) base to be designed and built as an air force installation and not converted from a previous army airfield. As a Strategic Air Command (SAC) premier installation, it was also one of the first to accommodate the B-36 Peacemaker bomber. The base was planned to accommodate 100 B-36 bombers, with the number of ramps, parking areas, weapons storage, and fuel capacities far exceeding later requirements. Planning of the installation was begun by the Army Corps of Engineers, New England Division, in June 1946 for a tract of land that was approximately 80 percent forest and 20 percent farmland.

Construction

The army authorized the initial construction of Limestone Army Airfield on April 5, 1947. Contracts for the multimillion-dollar construction project were awarded to Lane Construction Company of Meriden, Connecticut, and T.W. Cunningham, Inc., of Bangor, Maine. Construction began on April 15, 1947, and lasted until 1953. Limited funding, severe winters, and the enormous size of the project dictated that the base would have to be built in phases. The first phase called for the construction of a north–south runway, the arch hangar, the base operations building and control tower, an electric power plant, a railroad spur, barracks, and a water supply system. The passage of the National Security Act on September 18, 1947, initiated the dissolution of the War Department and the creation of a separate United States Air Force. Accordingly, the base's name shifted to Limestone Air Force Base, with a first-phase completion date scheduled for June 30, 1949.

The Korean conflict provided the catalyst for the second phase of construction at Limestone AFB, and drove increased funding from Congress; however, USAF Headquarters determined that Limestone AFB needed to begin limited operations with the first aircraft landing at Limestone AFB on June 12, 1950. Weeks later, on July 1, the 4215th Base Service Squadron was activated to administer the base as it gained increased operational capacity.

Construction at the base accelerated in 1951. The original 300 × 9,160-foot (91 × 2,792-m) runway was extended to 10,000 feet (3,048 m), and eight Luria maintenance hangars were constructed in the vicinity of the arch hangar. Other construction completed by 1952 included a base hospital, motor pool, communications facility, officers' club, and additional barracks.

Operational Storage Site "Easy" / Caribou Air Force Station / East Loring

On August 4, 1951, construction began in the northeastern corner of the base on a maximum-security storage area for atomic (and later, thermonuclear) weapons. This location was an Operational Storage Site (OSS) designated Site "Easy" (the phonetic representation at the time of the letter "E"). Site Easy was a "mini base," entirely self-sufficient, and included barracks, recreational facilities, offices, warehouses, weapon maintenance areas, and twenty-eight thermonuclear storage igloos. The site was officially named Caribou Air Force Station (AFS) in 1953, operating under the authority of the Air Materiel Command (AMC), with its sole mission was to protect and maintain strategic weapons used by SAC, and the 42d Bombardment Wing at Loring "next door." In July 1962, the Atomic Energy Commission transferred ownership and control of the stored thermonuclear weapons to SAC. Caribou AFS' real estate was renamed "East Loring," and was reassigned under the control of the 23d Munitions Maintenance Squadron. To facilitate rapid loading of the special weapons, a road connected East Loring directly to the rear entrance of the bomber alert area.

The 42d Bombardment Wing

On February 8, 1953, Commander-in-Chief, Strategic Air Command (CINCSAC) General Curtis Emerson LeMay visited Loring AFB, and satisfied with the progress, he indicated the base was ready for full operation. A week later, command of the air base was transferred from the U.S. Army Corps of Engineers (USACE) to SAC while awaiting the activation of the base's host organization.

The 42d Bombardment Wing (42 BMW) was activated and assumed host responsibilities at Limestone AFB on February 25, 1953, and was assigned to the Eighth Air Force. During March 1953, maintenance crews began preparing for full-scale B-36 operations, with the 69th Bombardment Squadron receiving ten B-36 bombers in April 1953. While awaiting aircraft and aircrew members, flying personnel flew training missions and handled deployments of other B-36 units. By the end of August 1953, the 69th, 70th, and 75th Bombardment Squadrons received their full complement of twenty-seven B-36 bombers and wing personnel grew to 322 officers, 313 airmen, and 350 civilians. On January 7, 1954, the 42 BMW declared full operational capability to implement their responsibilities within SAC's Emergency War Plan (renamed in the 1960s as the Single Integrated Operational Plan, or SIOP).

The following year, the base was officially redesignated as Loring AFB in honor of Major Charles J. Loring, a Maine native and posthumous Medal of Honor recipient recognized for deliberately crashing his crippled aircraft into North Korean enemy gun emplacements to protect his fellow pilots. In October 1954, SAC headquarters activated the 45th Air Division at Loring AFB and the USAF identified the base as the primary staging location for jet fighter aircraft flying between the United States and Europe, boosting transient air traffic. In July 1955, the mission of the bomb wing was expanded with the activation of the 42d Air Refueling Squadron (AREFS) and the arrival of twenty-one KC-97 piston-engine tankers.

Stratofortresses and Stratotankers Arrives

Preparations to receive the B-52 Stratofortress were underway in September 1955. Changing mission requirements saw the deactivation of the 75th Bomb Squadron in October 1955, leaving only two bomb squadrons at the base. On June 16, 1956, the first operational B-52 (C-model) arrived at Loring AFB and was christened the *State of Maine*. By September, Loring AFB had acquired twenty of the forty-five new aircraft to be assigned to the base. The first KC-135 Stratotanker arrived in December 1957. The KC-135s replaced the propeller-driven KC-97s, and the 42d AREFS was now capable of joining the 42 BMW mission of sustaining long-range bombardment and refueling capabilities worldwide. After receiving the first operational B-52C and KC-135A model aircraft in the U.S. inventory, the 42 BMW and 42d AREFS became the first all-jet, bomber-tanker combat unit in SAC, exemplifying the wing and base's status as SAC's nuclear vanguard.

Nuclear Alert at Loring

During the early days of SAC, nuclear deterrence operations and war planning were considered in terms of days and weeks. In the 1950s, the Soviet Union made technological advances with long-range bombers and atomic weapons, forcing the USAF to prepare for an unexpected attack. The Loring AFB alert force was established in October 1957 to defend against a surprise attack destroying retaliatory forces. Bomber aircrews moved into a temporary facility that was nearly 1 mile (1.6 km) from their awaiting alert aircraft. With long-range attack times lessening to mere hours, SAC eventually moved aircraft and aircrews into a specially designed bomber alert facility east of the southern end of the runway in 1960. An alert apron, with a design known as the crow's foot or "Christmas tree," was built next to the alert facility to keep the B-52s and KC-135s in proximity to the air crews. This layout allowed aircrews to reach their aircraft in minutes in response to an emergency or during operational readiness inspection (ORI) drills, saving valuable time.

After the development of intercontinental ballistic missiles (ICBMs), attack times were reduced to fractions of hours. SAC revised its response with the creation of minimum interval takeoff (MITO), in which aircraft took off in fifteen-second intervals, and the airborne alert force. The former allowed five alert aircraft to become airborne in under three minutes, while the latter kept a portion of the nuclear deterrent force airborne twenty-four hours a day. Airborne alert was maintained until 1968, when it was finally phased out due to the increased capability of the ICBM alert force and the high material cost and accident rate due to maintaining the airborne alert mission. While the airborne alert mission ended, ground alert continued until the end of the Cold War.

Loring's Air Defense Interceptors

In October 1959, the 27th Fighter Interceptor Squadron (27 FIS), a tenant unit belonging to the Air Defense Command, arrived equipped with the F-106 Delta Dart interceptors. The addition of interceptor aircraft at Loring provided increased defense capabilities for the Bangor Air Defense Sector and the northeastern United States. During the October 1962 Cuban Missile Crisis, the 27 FIS dispersed one-third of its force to Olmsted AFB (Pennsylvania), along with nuclear-tipped AIR-2A Genie rockets. This dispersal force returned to Loring after the crisis, and 27 FIS continued its air defense mission until 1 July 1971, when it was replaced by the 83d Fighter Interceptor Squadron (83 FIS), until its inactivation nearly a year later in June 1972.

The interceptor mission continued through the 1970s and 1980s with various units sending aircraft to Loring's alert hangars. The 5th Fighter Interceptor Squadron (5 FIS) maintained a detachment of three F-15 Eagles on alert until 1987, briefly replaced by F-4 Phantom IIs from the 179 Fighter Interceptor Squadron (179 FIS) from the Minnesota Air National Guard. The final interceptors came from the 101st Fighter Interceptor Squadron (101 FIS) fleet of F-15s from the Massachusetts Air National Guard until 1992.

Continued Alerts, the Cuban Missile Crisis, and the Vietnam War

During the early 1950s, the Eisenhower administration began development of the ADM-20 Quail decoy and AGM-28 Hound Dog nuclear-tipped air-launched missiles to help extend the reach of the B-52 Stratofortress into enemy airspace. Loring squadrons received Hound Dog missiles and Quail decoys between December 1960 and June 1961. The 42d Airborne Missile Maintenance Squadron (AMMS) was activated at Loring AFB on November 1, 1962, providing specialized maintenance for its Hound Dog and Quail force.

During October 1962, the U.S. discovered the Soviet Union building launch sites for nuclear-capable missiles on the island nation of Cuba, with range distances that would threaten U.S. military installations throughout the Continental United States. In response to this provocation, President John F. Kennedy ordered a naval blockade and air surveillance over Cuba. SAC's airborne alert force was increased and bombers and interceptors were dispersed around the country.

Loring joined other bases around the United States, with increased airborne alert missions and increased readiness, with the 42 BMW participating in "Hard Head" and "Chrome Dome," B-52 operations over the North Atlantic and the Mediterranean respectively. Units and their personnel went on twelve-hour shifts, seven days a week, for the duration of the forty-day crisis.

During the early 1970s, the U.S. military's continued participation in the Vietnam Conflict saw 42 BMW crews deploy to the Pacific for aerial bombardment missions. Notably, one Loring aircrew ("BRASS-02") flying B-52G (s/n 57-6481) was shot down on December 20, 1972 during Operation Linebacker II. The aircraft lost all electrical power from surface-to-air missile shrapnel and glided toward Nakhon Phanom air base for nearly forty minutes. All six crewmembers were rescued, five by search-and-rescue assets, with the sixth crewman taking a cab to the base's front gate.

Modernization of the Nuclear Arsenal

During the 1970s and 1980s, the 42 BMW continued to receive state-of-the-art weapons technology for integration into the arsenal of the B-52. Along with upgrades to the B-52G to include the AN/ASQ-151 electro-optical viewing system (EVS), notable offensive systems added to the arsenal were the AGM-69A short-range attack missile (SRAM), the AGM-84 Harpoon anti-ship missile, and the Mark 60 CAPTOR (captive torpedo) mine.

The 42 BMW became the first to operate these weapons based on Loring's strategic position as the northernmost base in the continental United States, and likely the first retaliatory force to reach the Soviet Union during a nuclear conflict. Loring crews integrated the SRAMs into its alert force by September 1972, and gained the first Harpoon-modified B-52 in September 1983, with full operational capability by 1984. Loring crews also became the first to deploy B-52s to Moron Air Base, Spain, in October 1983, re-energizing the bomber enterprise in Europe and laying the groundwork for future aerial operations. These weapons helped transition the mission of the 42 BMW to maintaining a B-52 force capable of short-notice, long-range bombing worldwide, strategic sea surveillance and reconnaissance, aerial minelaying, and Harpoon anti-ship missile operations. For the men and women of Loring AFB, the gauntlet was thrown, and the challenge was met with gusto.

Efforts to close Loring began in 1976. The USAF's rationale at that time was the poor condition of Loring AFB's facilities, and it was estimated the base needed up to $300 million ($1.6 billion in 2023 dollars) in facility improvements. Considerable debate over the strategic importance of Loring AFB took place between 1976 and 1979, resulting in the USAF reversing their decision to close the base. After the reversal, and with strong advocacy by Maine's representatives, Congress committed itself to upgrading the base facilities. In one clear case—the completion of a second runway in 1985—Loring became one of only three SAC bases to possess two fully capable runways, with ramp space exceeding 1.1 million square yards. This boosted the base to second among all SAC bases of total ramp space and first in excess ramp space. Additional numbers boosting Loring's value to the force included: weapons storage capacity of 10,247,882 NEW (net explosive weight)—highest in all of SAC; one of two fully capable conventional weapons storage facilities; and first in all of SAC with total fuel storage capacity (9,193,374 gallons).

Desert Shield/Desert Storm

After the invasion of Kuwait on August 2, 1990, the United States military planned a multi-coalition defense of the Arabian Peninsula with the build-up phase (Desert Shield) and the conflict phase (Desert Storm). Loring became a centerpiece in the transatlantic deployment effort, with KC-135 units refueling aircraft across the "pond," and ground personnel servicing aircraft departing the Continental U.S. Loring's B-52G aircrews and maintenance personnel were sent to join other BUFF wings with the creation of "provisional" (temporary) bomb wings at Diego Garcia (British Island Ocean Territory), Moron Air Base (Spain), and King Abdul Aziz International Airport (Saudi Arabia). During the build-up, however, the USAF inactivated the 407th AREFS, leaving Loring with only one refueling squadron: the 42 AREFS.

The overwhelming success during Desert Storm and the end of the Cold War led to a drawdown of military forces and divestiture of excess real estate and infrastructure. By 1991, the secretary of defense identified bases for closure, and Loring Air Force Base was one of the six SAC bases on the closure list. The Base Realignment and Closure (BRAC) commission projected net savings to the Department of Defense of $182 million by the end of 1997, or about $61.8 million annually. SAC itself was also a casualty of the changing geopolitical situation and was disestablished on June 1, 1992. For a brief time, Loring and the 42 BMW was administratively controlled under Air Combat Command (ACC), a USAF major flying command that inherited a portion of SAC's mission and assets. Celebratory ceremonies were held in February 1994 recognizing the end of the Loring's flying mission, though the last B-52 departed Loring in November 1993. The final KC-135 departed on March 2, 1994, and on September 30, 1994, Loring AFB officially closed.

Loring Post Closure

The Loring Development Authority created the Loring Commerce Center on a portion of the air base, housing various services, such as educational, engineering, food processing, forestry operations, light manufacturing, and aviation services. The 2005 Base Realignment and Closure Commission consolidated the military's Defense Finance and Accounting Service's (DFAS) twenty-six offices into five locations, with Loring's DFAS personnel working out of the old base hospital. The excessive ramp space was used twice during the 1990s and once in the early 2000s by the Vermont alternative rock band Phish. Their concerts brought in such high numbers of attendees that Loring became one of the largest "cities" in the state during the festivals. In 1998, 4,700 acres were transferred to the Fish and Wildlife Service to create the Aroostook National Wildlife Refuge.

Today, the legacy of Loring AFB and the men and women of the 42 BMW continue to echo throughout the state of Maine and the annals of United States Air Force history.

THE SKIES FOR US: The heraldic emblem for the 42d Bombardment Wing is described as: on a bend engrailed or, four annulets gules, between two aerial bombs palewise of the second, all within a diminutive bordure of the last. The emblem was approved for 42d Group on March 11, 1942, and again for 42d Bombardment Wing, Heavy on April 16, 1954. The motto of the 42d Bomb Wing is *AETHERA NOBIS* ("The skies for us").

AERIAL WARRIOR: A Maine native, Charles Joseph Loring, Junior was born on October 2, 1918, in Portland (ME). Enlisting in the U.S. Army Air Forces in March 1942, the twenty-three-year-old Loring became an aviation cadet and earned his commission as a second lieutenant on February 16, 1943. His first assignment was with the 22d Fighter Squadron/36th Fighter Group defending the Panama Canal and Caribbean islands. The group converted to the P-47 Thunderbolt (seen above behind Loring) in early 1944, prepared for aerial combat and ground support using the aircraft's eight 0.50-in (12.7-mm) machine guns. In April 1944, the 36 FG transferred to English to support Operation Overlord, the invasion of Europe. By December 1944, Loring had flown fifty-five combat missions in his P-47 Thunderbolt (s/n 44-19864), earning the Distinguished Flying Cross for the destruction of ten German armored vehicles. On December 24, 1944, Loring was shot down over Hotten, Belgium, and spent the next six months as a German prisoner of war.

1

Major Charles Joseph Loring, Jr.

While leading a flight of four F-80 aircraft on a close support mission, Maj. Charles J. Loring was briefed by a controller to dive-bomb enemy gun positions that were harassing friendly ground troops. After verifying the location of the target, Maj. Loring rolled into his dive-bomb run, immediately receiving extremely accurate ground fire aimed at his aircraft. Disregarding the accuracy and intensity of the ground fire, Maj. Loring aggressively continued to press the attack until his aircraft was hit. At approximately 4,000 feet, he intentionally altered his course and aimed his diving aircraft at active gun emplacements concentrated on a ridge northwest of the briefed target, turned his aircraft 45 degrees to the left, pulled up in a deliberate, controlled maneuver, and elected to sacrifice his life by diving his aircraft directly into the midst of the enemy emplacements. His selfless and heroic action destroyed the enemy gun emplacement and eliminated a dangerous threat to United Nations ground forces. Maj. Loring's noble spirit, superlative courage, and conspicuous self-sacrifice in inflicting maximum damage on the enemy exemplified valor of the highest degree, and his actions were in keeping with the finest traditions of the U.S. Air Force.

A MAINE HERO IS LOST: Major Loring watches his pilots take off, while serving as the 80th Fighter-Bomber Squadron operations officer. On April 17, 1954, President Dwight Eisenhower presented the Congressional Medal of Honor (MoH) posthumously to Mrs. Elsie Colton Loring, Maj. Loring's widow. The award of the MoH took place on May 5, 1953, but was withheld from public notice to protect him from enemy reprisal as Loring was still listed as missing in action. His wife later stated "[Charley] held a great regard for the ground troops," telling her "I've got a soft spot in my heart for the infantry. I'd do anything for them." Loring's sacrifice is also hinted in a quote from his father, "Charley was a stubborn man. He said he would never be a prisoner again. He was the kind of man who kept his word about everything." Secretary of the Air Force Harold E. Talbott shows the MoH to Maj. Loring's children, Aldor (5) and Charlene (4).

2

The Air Base Near Limestone, Maine

In the summer of 1947, routine life in the little town of Limestone, Maine—nestled among the gently rolling hills of Aroostook County—was disrupted by the thunder of heavy equipment as construction started on the nearby Limestone Army Airfield.

FARMLAND AS FAR AS THE EYE CAN SEE: Originally named Limestone Army Airfield during its initial planning phases, the base was renamed Limestone Air Force Base in September 1947 after the establishment of the United States Air Force as a separate military service. Above, the photo looks toward the east gate of the air base from the junction of Corrow Road and Grass School Road in June 1948. The site in Aroostook County was selected for a variety of reasons: shortened routes over the Arctic Circle to targets in the Soviet Union, cheap land, and plentiful construction materials such as bedrock and limestone. Since being introduced to the area in the early 1800s, potatoes quickly became a cash crop, with Aroostook County continuing as one of the nation's largest provider and exporter of the starchy food. Farms such as these became neighbors to the air base and its many construction projects in the community.

MOVING HEAVEN AND PLENTY OF EARTH: Thousands of felled trees were cleared during runway construction, *c.* August 1947. Looking north from the southern end of the runway along the approximate centerline gives a brief indication of how large the concrete landing path is going to be post-construction. The clearing for the spur track runs along the bottom of the photo, while the parking apron's future location is in the upper right. The opposite perspective shows the camera looking south from the north end of the airfield nearly a month after the top photograph, in early September 1948.

THE HEART OF ANY AIR BASE: Limestone AFB's base operations and air traffic control tower clock as shown during early base construction and with an artist's concept illustration. The clock face on the tower is a one-of-a-kind feature that was quoted in the Limelight base paper as being "a real oddity." From a distance and a quick glance, nothing seems afoot. However, closer inspection reveals the entire face of the clock was made of scrap lumber, with the minute hand being nothing more than an old rake handle. The person responsible for the clock's construction was Harry L. Olmstead from Limestone, Maine. Olmstead oversaw all construction on the air base from 1947 until his retirement in 1967.

MAINE'S SNOWY DAYS: Aroostook County's location in the northern tier of the United States means that many days of the year snow will fall, and fall ... and fall. SAC's placement of bomber and ICBM bases in the far northern states presumed operations would not be deterred by weather. The Bangor and Aroostook Railroad locomotive pushes a wedge plow through snow near Limestone AFB. The face of the plow allowed snow to slip past the moving vehicle and away from the tracks, rather than compressing the snow in front of the engine. A vehicle sits alongside a cleared road at Loring AFB on March 30, 1959. During the air base's early construction, the U.S. Army Corps of Engineers (USACE) New England District had a constant presence, as the rear hood markings on this car show. In the back window is a USACE white helmet adorned with the corps' distinct castle emblem.

WOODEN ARCHES FOR FREEDOM: The construction of the arch hangar was a watershed moment in air force history. Designed by the Roberts and Schaefer Company of Chicago, the arch hangar was the first structure built by SAC to directly support the mission of nuclear deterrence, shielding two massive B-36 bombers from the elements. Displayed in the civil engineer's office, the "thin slice" working model of the hangar's parabolic arch design shows intimate details of the building's internals. The model shows how the footings extend out from the structure, along with the absence of any internal support structures inside the massive building. The concrete footings were massive, measuring 8 × 35 feet and reaching a height of 7 feet, and set into limestone bedrock at a depth of 22 feet below the floor level.

THOUSANDS OF FEET OF CONSTRUCTION LUMBER: Wooden scaffolding provided workers an internal support structure during the construction of the arch hangar. At the time of construction, the design of the arch hangar met the military's requirements for an unobstructed space of 340 × 300 feet and provided maximum fire resistance at minimum cost. The use of reinforced concrete for construction was the most economical method at the time because the formwork could be effectively reused in pouring the arches. Designers also hoped that the same equipment could be used in building other arch hangars on Limestone AFB and other SAC installations. Due to changes in SAC force structure (namely the elimination of the B-36 in favor of the B-52) and additional costs of lighting and heating in Maine's climate, no additional arch hangar-like structures were built. Austrian engineer Anton Tedesko pioneered the use of thin-shell concrete in the United States, reaching the technological pinnacle with the two nearly identical military aircraft hangars built in Rapid City, SD (Ellsworth AFB) and Limestone, ME (Loring AFB) during 1948.

A LITTLE BIT OF SCALE PROVIDES A LOT OF CONTEXT: The man climbing the wooden safety staircase provides a sense of scale to the enormity of the arch hangar's 90-foot height and 340-foot span, *c.* June 1948. In the early 1930s, engineer Anton Tedesko worked with the Chicago firm of Roberts and Schaefer (R&S) promoting the use of thin shell concrete roofs. During World War II and the years following, Tedesko designed several long-spanning thin shell concrete roofs to serve as aircraft hangars, with the 340-foot span used at Ellsworth AFB and Loring AFB as the longest spanning shells. While massive in size, these concrete shells were only 5 inches thick. The importance of the arch hangar is exemplified here, as the structure is nearing completion in September 1948 during construction Phase 1, along with the north-south runway, taxiway, parking apron, base operations, power plant, barracks, water supply, and a railroad spur.

Loring's Other Large Hangar: Construction workers placed miles of steel reinforcing bars before the concrete floor of the huge double cantilever (DC) hangar was ready to be poured in the summer of 1955. Loring's other cavernous structure, the DC hangar, was designed to provide maximum usable space while minimizing construction costs. During early construction, 260 concrete caissons were shot into the Earth with a 7,000-lb hydraulic ram, resting 25 feet below the surface atop a limestone formation. Completed on November 3, 1954, the 250 × 600-foot hangar enclosed nearly 194,247 sq. feet, surpassing the space provided under the arch hangar. Maj.-Gen. Sir Eustice F. Tickell, the chief engineer at the British War Office (left), visits the air base construction site with Brigadier General R. C. Moses (right), engineer with USACE's New England Division, on June 4, 1948.

LIMESTONE'S SOCIAL "WATERING HOLE": Two unidentified young women enjoy a drink at the Limestone Army Airfield canteen on April 14, 1948, as a box of waffle ice cream cones sits behind the counter. The canteen offered respite for base construction workers and civilians assigned to prepare the base for operation. Later social gathering places on base included the officers' club for commissioned officers and their families, the non-commissioned officers' (NCO) club for enlisted families, and the youth center for base children. The canteen dining room shows the austere nature of the facility during the construction years. The tables are nothing more than standard American picnic tables brought indoors, with condiments and napkin dispensers placed atop. The rear of the dining room has merchandise cases for sales of comfort items to weary workers.

3

Cold War in Aroostook County

While Limestone AFB officially became operational on February 23, 1953, Col. Bertram C. Harrison welcomed the local communities to the base's 1953 Open House held on August 3, 1953. Harrison stands in front of a lectern with the WAGM radio call letters, a local AM station broadcasting to Presque Isle and Caribou, as dignitaries and a band look on. Open Houses were common throughout the Cold War years on many military bases, allowing the public to see what their tax dollars were paying for. Many future military members recall youthful experiences touring around aircraft and base buildings, cementing their desires to join the military.

HEMISPHERICAL DEFENSE PIONEERED AT LIMESTONE: The first aircraft type programmed for Limestone AFB was the B-36 Peacemaker, a long-range nuclear bomber. The first B-36s to land at Limestone AFB arrived on June 16, 1950. Two B-36s from Carswell AFB, Texas, stopped by the Maine air base during a training flight helmed by Col. Thomas Gerrity, the commander of the 11th Bombardment Group. After a brief layover, the pair of B-36s refueled and departed, circling over Presque Isle and Fort Fairfield before returning to their Texas air base that evening. B-36s were critical to the post-war "Hemisphere Defense" strategy with a 10,000-mile range carrying an approximately 87,000-lb bomb load without the need for landing and refueling. The KC-97 aerial refueling tanker was an evolutionary outgrowth of the KB-29M (hose-type) and KB-29P (boom) tankers. The flying boom used a telescoping tube with two "ruddervator" control surfaces to fly the boom into the receptacle on the receiving aircraft. Additional space inside the KC-97 allowed crews to move large amounts of cargo in addition to its aerial refueling mission.

ALUMINUM OVERCAST ON A CLOUDY MAINE DAY: This wistfully ironic image shows the 42d Air Refueling Squadron's KC-97 tankers near B-36 bombers that were not designed for aerial refueling. This deficiency, as well as its slower overall speed compared to all-jet bombers, helped reinforce the B-36's obsolescence to supporting nuclear weapon delivery. Limestone AFB was the first installation designed specifically for Strategic Air Command's mission of strategic deterrence, housing the enormous B-36 bomber, due to the geographic location at the northeastern edge of continental U.S. territory. The addition of KC-97 tankers gave the base increased importance by providing additional range to intercontinental aircraft transiting to and from northeastern U.S., which held true into the B-52 and KC-135 era. The Luria all-aluminum nose dock hangars, pictured below, allowed the front of aircraft and their engines to be worked on under cover from weather, while the tail sections projected outside the hangars. In the extreme right rear of the photo, another B-36 sits outside, exposed to the elements.

FOOD THAT FUELS THE FORCE: This image shows a lunchroom at Limestone AFB in 1953. While commonplace today, this moment captures the scene five years after the desegregation of the U.S. military. President Harry S. Truman signed Executive Order 9981 on July 26, 1948, calling for the desegregation of the U.S. Armed Forces, ending 170 years of officially sanctioned discrimination. From the image, the Black airmen in their service dress enjoy the same level of respect with shared accommodations alongside their White peers. An unidentified cafeteria worker poses beside the Limestone lunch menu, displaying such fare as ham ($0.25), egg salad ($0.20), and cheese ($0.15) sandwiches along with soup ($0.20), chili ($0.30), and beef stew ($0.35), with the temptation of trying Sealtest ice cream products.

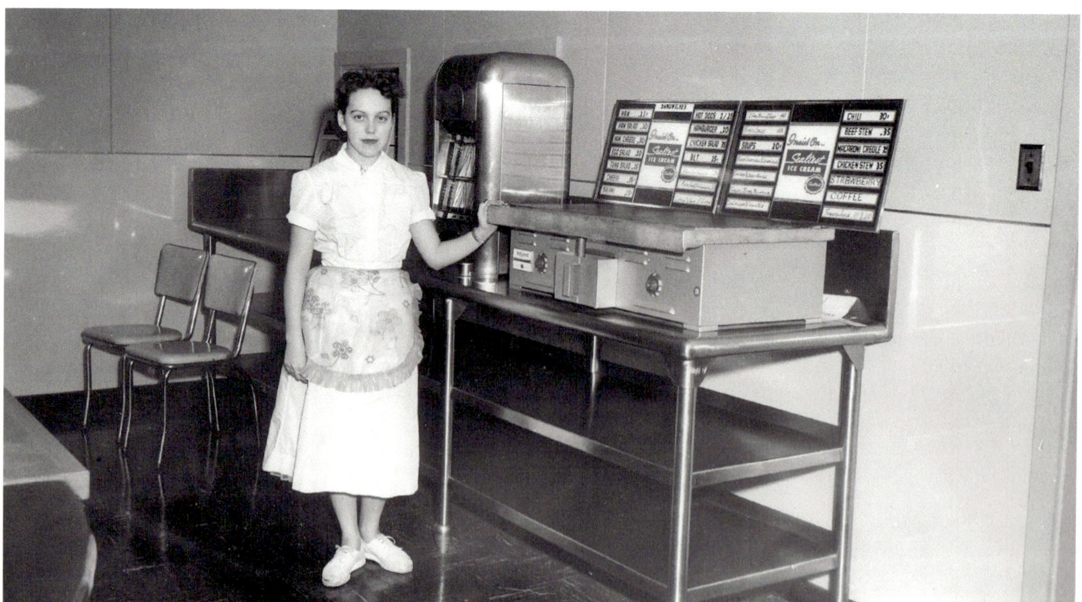

PRÊT-À-PORTER COMES TO THE PINE TREE STATE: Invited guests walk down passenger boarding stairs at Loring AFB, while smiling and waving to the crowd. Two dozen smartly dressed fashion models gave a presentation on February 13, 1955, to nearly 1,200 air force members and their spouses. The special exhibition came from the *Boston Herald*'s fashion show, complete with an elaborate Caribbean resort setting on display at the frozen Maine air base. Models walk along a runway inside the base gymnasium while presenting the latest New England chic clothing items.

WAFs ON THE BASKETBALL COURT: Loring AFB hosted the Northeast Area Air Force Sports Conference Women in the Air Force (WAF) basketball tournament February 21–25, 1955. Nearly 1,500 airmen watched ten WAF teams compete at Limestone during the weeklong event. One hundred and twenty women representing their units from Andrews AFB (D.C.), Fort Myer (VA), Mitchel AFB (NY), Westover AFB (MA), Otis AFB (MA), Sampson AFB (NY), Roslyn AFB (NY), Hancock Field (NY), Stewart AFB (NY), and a WAF group from Bethesda (MD). The winning team members—the Sampson Sabrettes—were awarded camera kits, while the second-place team from Otis AFB were presented with traveling clocks. Major Frank Wrigglesworth presents the winner's trophy to Mary Moore, captain of the Sabrettes.

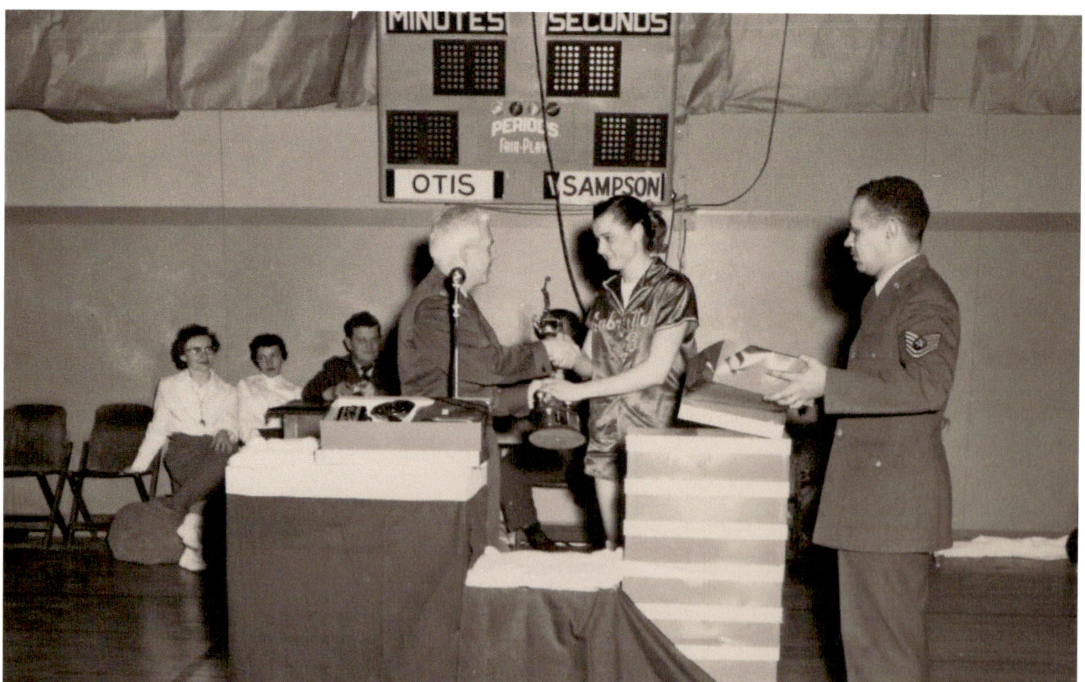

KEY FIGURES VISIT LIMESTONE FOR A LOOK-SEE: Maj.-Gen. Walter C. Sweeney, Eighth Air Force commanding general, steps out of a C-97 transport at Loring AFB. On April 15, 1956, Sweeney presided over a world premier showing of *Assignment in Aroostook*, a film depicting the experiences of a young sergeant and his family in Maine, produced by the Bangor and Aroostook Railroad. The premier event also treated the audience to a fifteen-act variety show, "Rhythm in Blue," from Westover AFB (ME). Days later, Sweeney hosted Nebraska Governor Victor Anderson and thirty members of the Omaha Chamber of Commerce at Loring. The group previously toured Portsmouth AFB (NH), investigating New England's air bases supporting Strategic Air Command, which was headquartered in Omaha (NE).

RECOGNIZING THE MEN AND WOMEN OF THE 45TH AIR DIVISION: The men and women of Loring AFB pass in review before Brig.-Gen. Bertram C. Harrison, outgoing 45th Air Division commander on June 18, 1955. Harrison (next to the microphone) stands for the review of troops flanked by key staff officers. Harrison's command was not remembered fondly by one enlisted aircrew member: "[Harrison] decided that [Loring] base personnel lacked discipline, and devised several means to re-establish it.... such as installing loud speakers around the base and play reveille [at 6 a.m.] and march music the balance of the day. [On Saturdays] everyone had to report to the base briefing center to listen to lectures ranging from catching the 'clap' [gonorrhea, a sexually transmitted infection] to safety, then practice marching drills to march music played by a record player sitting on top of a flatbed trailer."

THE 1956 SAC BOMB COMP AT LORING AFB: A B-36 and its aircrew is greeted on the ramp by the Loring AFB mobile base exchange (BX) and snack bar during the 1956 SAC Bombing and Navigation Competition. The competition was established by SAC's first commander General George Kenney, to improve the bombing accuracy of his aircrew members. The first bomb competition was held at Castle AFB (CA) in June 1948. Loring AFB hosted crews from B-36 and B-52 wings during the 1956 competition, while the remaining B-47 medium bombers were hosted at Lockbourne AFB (OH). An unidentified female employee motions to the "Pride First" motto emblazoned on the mobile snack bar, as adjacent military members enjoy a cup of hot coffee. When aircrews were unable to leave the runway for trips to the BX for sundries or food, the mobile units would drive out to them.

JUST ANOTHER DAY ON LORING: Judges for the 1956 SAC Bombing and Navigation Competition sit in the Loring AFB control tower. Each crew flew three missions consisting of three radar bombing scoring runs (at 33,000 feet), along with a night leg via celestial navigation. The 1956 comp was the first to combine navigation, bombing, and reconnaissance and included the debut of the B-52 Stratofortress. Damon Elementary School was officially renamed on December 10, 1954 after one of Limestone's citizens, Dr. A. H. Damon. The thirty-one-room building originally housed 620 students from first through seventh grades and cost $873,000 ($9.8M in 2023). The initial school design came from Alonzo H. Harriman, Inc. (Auburn, ME) and was built by Consolidated Constructors, Inc. of Portland (ME). Brigadier General Bertram C. Harrison, commander of the 45th Air Division and Congressman Clifford G. McIntire (R-ME) gave speeches at the dedication ceremony. The school originally opened on September 28, 1953.

THE BEST IN SAC ARE RECOGNIZED: On January 7, 1959, Lieutenant Colonel Willis H. Sonnteg (center), commander of the 42d Air Refueling Squadron hoists the "Golden Boom" trophy, with 45th Air Division commander Colonel S. W. Wells (left), and 42d Bomb Wing commander Colonel J. W. Gaff, Jr. (right) looking on. The Golden Boom was presented each month to the most efficient Air Refueling Squadron in the Eighth Air Force. In February 1956, Loring AFB earned the SAC Flying Safety Award (below). From left to right: Captain F. J. Williams, wing flying safety officer; Lieutenant Colonel David C. Jolly, director of operations; Major Keith M. Garrison, editor of SAC's *Combat Crew Magazine*; Brigadier General W. K. Martin, 45th Air Division commander; Colonel Jackson W. Lewis, 42d Air Base Group commander; Captain Leonard Levandowski, director of safety; and Major R. T. Mattingly, deputy director of operations.

Kids Growing up at Loring: Dependent children of military personnel enjoy a boat ride at the Loring AFB Recreation Camp at Long Lake in June 1956, while cabins and the boat dock can be seen in the background. In 1960, a raid by the state liquor inspectors and subsequent seizure of seventy-two cases of beer from Staff Sergeant Robert L. Zeh at Long Lake Recreation Center was later deemed illegal by a federal judge. The sale of alcohol had been under a non-appropriated fund activity on federal property, and highlights close connection between airmen, their alcohol, and accomplishing the air force mission, along with the means they will undertake to get their beer back. Long Lake was a popular spot for Loring families to enjoy summer and winter camping activities.

HELPING OUT OUR NEIGHBORS TO THE NORTH:

On Sunday April 8, 1956, a fire broke out in the heart of the Grand Falls (N.B.) business district, causing over $50,000 in damages and the death of a twelve-year-old Canadian boy, Maurice Therriault. The Loring AFB Fire Department provided two fire engines, an ambulance, and an unknown number of military personnel to assist in the Grand Falls firefighting efforts. Loring members assist in raising a ladder in front of Frank P. Cote's jewelry store while fighting the downtown Grand Falls blaze, while two exhausted Loring military members take over firehose duties during the blaze.

AIR FORCE TELEVISION'S FIRST STATION: Staff Sergeant Barry Myers (at anchor desk) checks news copy before airtime, while Staff Sergeant Bob Dean (white overalls) readies the orthicon camera. During his tenure as Commander-in-Chief Strategic Air Command (CINCSAC) General Curtis E. LeMay noted the sparseness of entertainment options at isolated installations, including then-Limestone AFB. Progress on improving this was slow until Brigadier General David Sarnoff—with the aid of RCA—created Air Force Television (AF-TV). Limestone's station was the first AF-TV station and located inside a 40 × 13-foot tarpaper "penthouse" shack, complete with soundstage, cameras, and editing equipment, transmitting 8 watts of power to keep the signal within the base boundaries. The station's first telecast was *The Littlest Angel*, broadcast on Christmas Day 1953. Ten hours a day of AF-TV programming included popular shows of the time: *I Love Lucy*, *Dragnet*, *Toast of the Town*, *Comedy Hour*, and *TV Playhouse*. Staff Sergeant Arthur Hanlon, AF-TV engineer, checks out equipment, *c.* February 1955.

ARMED FORCES DAY SHOWS "POWER FOR PEACE": A carnival was set up inside the arch hangar for military dependents during Armed Forces Day, May 19, 1956. Loring personnel estimated over 100,000 visitors saw the themed "Power for Peace" program, with close-up views of static displays of aircraft and other military equipment. The Pipe and Drum Band of the First Battalion, The Black Watch (Royal Highland Regiment) of Canada, performed for spectators during the 1956 Armed Forces Day program. The Loring flight line displayed Navy F9F Panther, AD6 Skyraider, F2H Banshee, and P2V-7 Neptune, while the air force aircraft were the B-36 Peacemaker, B-50 Superfortress, KC-97 Stratofreighter, F-94 Starfire, F-89 Scorpion, and F-86 Sabrejet.

HOUSING THE FORCE: Capehart Housing undergoes construction at Loring AFB in the mid-1950s. While other bases had thousands of units constructed post World War II under the Wherry Program —named after the bill's sponsor Senator Kenneth Wherry (NE-R)—Limestone/Loring AFB was constructed closer to the timeframe of the Capehart Program (1955-1962). In 1950, President Harry S. Truman created the Defense Housing Commission to study the issue of housing military families and establish the Armed Forces Housing Agency. The Defense Housing Act, passed in 1954. and saw housing construction for approximately 18,000 homes. The following year, Congress authorized the Capehart Program, producing more than 115,000 houses, built on government land by private contractors under mortgages insured by the Federal Housing Administration. By 1964, when Capehart construction came to an end, approximately 250,000 units of both Wherry and Capehart were built at military installations; by the end of 1994, roughly 175,000 units were still in existence.

A PEACEMAKER DIES SLOWLY: B-36B-1 (B-36D) Peacemaker (s/n 44-92030), the twenty-seventh aircraft manufactured, crashed at Loring AFB on March 6, 1955. The aircraft caught fire after a wingtip hit a snowbank during landing, though all eleven crewmen walked away from the crash. Snowdrifts helped cushion the crash impact and held back the spread of fire. The crewmen of 44-92030: Captain George H. Bailey, aircraft commander; Captain Joseph R. Henry, pilot; Captain Alfred F. Hendrix, radio operator; First Lieutenant Milam L. Jackson, flight engineer; Master Sergeant John Gallagher, flight engineer; Technical Sergeant Raymond Wedro, radio operator; Master Sergeant Donald L. Johnson, gunner; Airman First Class Raymond G. Fitzgerald; Airman Second Class William Gray, gunner; Airman Second Class John F. Werbe, gunner; and Airman Third Class Arnold L. Dutton, gunner.

ENTER THE STRATOFORTRESS: January 9, 1956, marked the first visit of a B-52 Stratofortress to the East Coast of the United States. One of the first three B-52A models landed at Loring AFB following a three-hour flight from Eglin AFB (FL). The aircraft was undergoing Phase V all-weather testing, primarily at Wright Air Development Center (OH) and Eglin. While Eglin possessed the McKinley Climatic Laboratory, able to test weapon systems from negative 80 degrees to 165 degrees Fahrenheit, real-world testing at Loring helped show the weapon in its soon-to-be "natural" habitat. The aircraft's nose displays the logo of the Air Research and Development Command (ARDC), designating this B-52 as a test "bird." After the stop at Loring, the aircraft continued to Alaska for additional special cold weather testing. By this time, the 42d Bomb Wing was notified it would be the first operational SAC base to receive the B-52 Stratofortress, with the 69th, 70th, and 75th Bombardment Squadrons flying the B-52C model by the middle of the year.

4

Changing of the Guard

The Loring parking ramp shows two eras of air force technology, with the propeller-driven KC-97Gs in the rear, and an all-jet B-52C (s/n 54-2667) sitting in the foreground. The KC-97 was based on the Boeing Model 367, a military transport based on the B-29 Superfortress bomber. KC-97 tankers became crucial to SAC operations, extending the range of bombers and fighters. The first B-52C landed on June 16, 1956, and was subsequently christened *State of Maine*, bringing Loring's strategic deterrent force into the Jet Age.

PASSING GAS IN THE JET AGE: Loring received all thirty-five airframes of the B-52C variant in 1956, the smallest production run of the eight B-52 versions. The C-model introduced larger, 3,000-gallon under-wing fuel tanks and fixed the water-injection system issues from the B-models. The C-models did not remain at Loring long—by December 1956, all thirty-five aircraft had transferred to the 99th Bomb Wing at Westover AFB (MA) to make room for the B-52D model. The first KC-135A Stratotanker arrived at Loring AFB on October 16, 1957, with Major Willie H. Sonntag (aircraft commander); Major Henry Markow (pilot); Captain Judson B. Campbell, Jr. (navigator); Master Sergeant Edward E. Caldwell (boom operator); and Master Sergeant Kenneth B. Burrows (42 ARS maintenance chief). After landing, the aircraft subsequently christened *Aroostook Queen* by the pilot's wife, Mrs. Gladys Sonntag. Loring's 42d Air Refueling Squadron was the first tactical unit in SAC to receive the jet-powered aerial refueler. The A-model held approximately 30,000-gallons of JP-4 aviation fuel, with the ability to deliver 900 gallons a minute through the aerial refueling boom. The 42 ARS finished transitioning to the KC-135 at the end of the year, with the final KC-97 departing on December 20, 1957.

Loring Gets First Jet Tanker In Changeover From KC-97

$8,000,000 Craft Flies From Seattle

By JIM BARROWS

LORING A.F.B., Oct. 16—The first of Loring's new KC-135's wheeled low over a welcoming crowd here this afternoon just four hours after the new Air Force $8,000,000 tanker left Seattle.

Loring is the first strategic air command base to receive the Boeing-built Stratotanker for operational use in a tactical squadron.

Scheduled for use by the 42d Air Refueling Squadron, the KC-135's will eventually replace the propeller-driven KC-97's which are now in use at Loring.

FOUR HOURS FROM SEATTLE—Touching down at Loring Air Force Base in

THE SHOES AND STINGER OF THE STRATOFORTRESS: Maintainers move a tire into position while performing a tire replacement on a B-52 amidst typical New England snow. A typical landing gear tire change on a B-52 took over two hours in good weather conditions. The approximately 170,000-lb B-52 airframe requires lifting via tripod jacks during tire replacement. Below, the Stratofortress' "stinger"—four 0.50-caliber M-3 machine guns—undergo maintenance upkeep. As a holdover from World War II and Korean War aerial combat, all B-52 variants included machine guns for rear defensive capability. The A through F variants were equipped with the quad complement of 50-caliber guns (containing 600 rounds each) manned by a gunner in the tail. The G variant flown at Loring retained the four guns but moved the gunner into the main fuselage upper compartment next to the Electronic Warfare Officer (EWO). The final Stratofortress variant—the B-52H—replaced the quad guns with a 20-mm M61 Vulcan cannon. Due to changes in the adversary threat capability, and increased likelihood of being destroyed by air-to-air missiles, rear guns were removed from the B-52 fleet between 1991 and 1994.

Protect/Defend and Photograph/Document:

The silhouette of a 42d Combat Defense Squadron sentry and his military working dog is seen amongst shadows of B-52s on the Loring flight line. Concurrent to the buildup of SAC nuclear forces was the requirement for security requirements to guard the men, planes, and atomic/thermonuclear weapons. By 1955, the air force required hundreds of additional sentry dogs to augment the nearly 1,400 already on duty worldwide. Airman Second Class (A2C) James "Jim" Gildzyn works inside the base photo lab. In the present day, this function is performed by base public affairs photographers; however, during A2C Gildzyn's day, the Base Photo Lab oversaw documenting thousands of activities on Loring, from the mundane (photos for press releases) to the extraordinary (inside classified areas, or aircraft crashes and sometimes human remains) for archival purposes. A few of A2C Gildzyn's photographs are featured inside this book, closing a chapter on his amazing work at Loring AFB.

THE DELTA DART OVER (AND ATOP) MAINE: Boasting an impressive aerodynamic sleekness, this Convair F-106A Delta Dart (s/n 59-0038) belonged to the 27th Fighter Interceptor Squadron (27 FIS) while at Loring AFB. The F-106 was an all-weather interceptor assigned to the Air Defense Command, able to counter enemy aircraft up to 70,000 feet and catch nearly anything with its 1,525-mph (Mach 2.3) speed. It was armed with AIM-4 Falcon missiles for individual air-to-air interception, and one nuclear-tipped AIR-2 Genie rocket (with a 1.5-kiloton warhead) to disperse enemy bomber formations. Loring had a number of accidents involving the airframe, such as this one on May 18, 1968, with F-106 (s/n 59-0042). Capt. Francis J. Vyzral (1936–1977) attempted a barrier arrested landing after his landing gear malfunctioned during practice maneuvers for the 1968 Armed Forces Day open house at Loring. Vyzral performed a normal landing approach at nearly 165 miles per hour, and when his speed dropped, the aircraft's left wingtip struck the runway and flung the Delta Dart into a nearby grassy field. Sadly, Vyzral would lose his life in another aircraft accident at Fort Knox (KY) in 1977.

STRATOFORTRESS MAINTAINERS LEARN THEIR CRAFT, PART 1: An unidentified technical sergeant leads an on-the-job training class about the B-52's pneumatic system, with attentive students looking on. The visual aid displays the diagram of an RB-52B, due in no small part to the minimal internal changes from the RB-52B (which did not fly at Loring) to the B-52C, which the 42d Bomb Wing received in 1956. Two students are instructed on the crosswind capabilities of the B-52. The B-52 was created with the ability to offset its landing gear angle to match the directional heading of the runway, so the aircraft nose could be tilted away from the runway axis in high crosswind conditions.

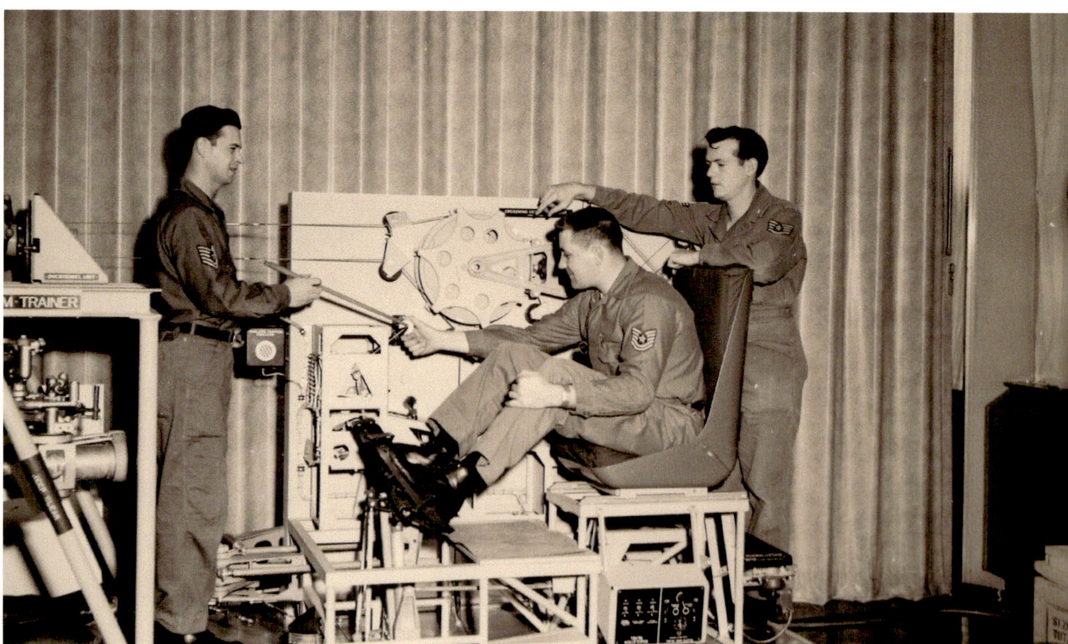

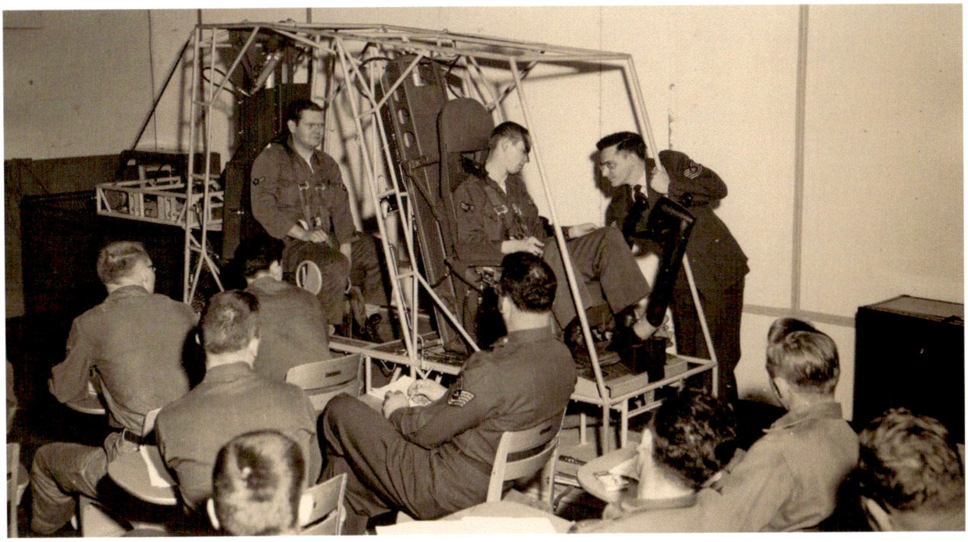

STRATOFORTRESS MAINTAINERS LEARN THEIR CRAFT, PART 2: Two Loring airmen second class (A2C) maintainers sit inside the B-52 ejection seat simulator during a class of instruction in March 1956. The B-52C Stratofortress emergency egress options were varied: the pilot and copilot had seats that fired upward, as did the electronic warfare officer (a.k.a. electronic countermeasure operator) on the upper deck. The bombardier-navigators (a.k.a. nav and radar nav) had seats that fired downward. The gunner positioned in the tail simply ejected the tail turret and jumped out. Later B-52G models moved the gunner inside the crew compartment, next to the EWO, with an upward ejection seat. Two maintainers inspect aviation electronics ("avionics") for the B-52. Boeing's company lore states the B-52 was created over a weekend in Dayton (OH) in 1948—complete with a balsa wood model—to convince the air force to build their aircraft design. The aircraft's increasing longevity gives credence its maintenance concept of Loring airmen such as these to "keep 'em flying" after nearly every conceivable problem or issue arises.

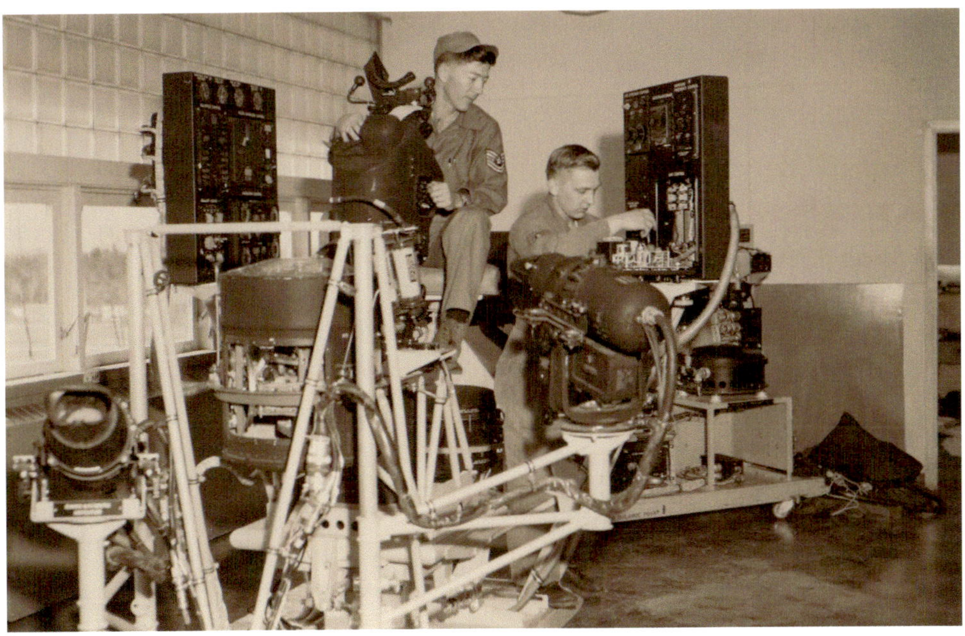

SAC's Ground Alert Force: Capt. James H. Spearman, Jr. (1918–1993) of the 70th Bombardment Squadron performs a final check on the outer gear door of his B-52C during ground alert at Loring AFB in July 1958. Note Capt. Spearman's pistol and holster, a common accoutrement for aircrew during early Cold War alerts. Ground alert was a basic tenet of SAC's deterrence strategy for decades, with a certain percentage of bombers and tankers standing ready to become airborne within fifteen minutes of warning. The crew of B-52G (s/n 57-6504) run toward their bomber during an alert drill. Note the aircraft armament of the port-side GAM-77 (later, AGM-28) Hound Dog supersonic standoff missile.

GETTING AIRBORNE BEFORE GETTING NUKED: The aircrew of B-52G (s/n 57-6504) perform their synchronized maneuvers to get the armament ready, engines started, and crew aboard during a ground alert exercise. While a few crew members pull "Remove Before Flight" tags, some climb aboard the aircraft to start the engines. In September 1960, SAC created the principle of minimum interval take-off (MITO) to launch all of a unit's aircraft in the least possible time. Prior to MITO, SAC crews were ordered to take off "as soon as possible." Gen. Thomas Power's establishment of MITO specified the last bomber would launch no later than fifteen minutes after notification of attack. A Hound Dog-laden Stratofortress could use the missile's engines for additional take-off thrust. After becoming airborne (and additional refueling), the B-52 crew would transfer fuel from the aircraft back into the missile.

LORING'S AIRBORNE SENTINELS: Flying over Maine's green forests, B-52G (s/n 57-6475) appears in early Cold War markings, with reflective metal and white panels along the fuselage, and the large "U.S. Air Force" along the side of the crew compartment. SAC began testing the airborne alert concept during the late 1950s, with Operation Head Start II (March 2–June 30, 1959) always keeping five B-52 bombers in the air performing 24-hour sorties with support from ten KC-135A tankers. An early model B-52 (possibly B-52C) prepares for refueling from the KC-135A (s/n 55-3127). At the rear of the Stratotanker, note the aerial boom's black "ruddervators" and extension looking like an insect's proboscis.

SAC's Premier Stratofortress and Stratotanker Drivers: From the 42d Bomb Wing's original three bombardment squadrons—the 69th, 70th, and 75th—only the 69th remained after the 70th was deactivated in 1966. The 42d Air Refueling Squadron (42 AREFS) was activated in 1955 and was originally equipped with KC-97G Stratofreighter until October 1957, when KC-135A Stratotankers arrived. The 42d AREFS was met with the arrival of the 407th AREFS in July 1968, doubling the strength of the wing's aerial refueling fleet until the 407 AFRES inactivation in October 1990. Both the 69 BS and 42 AFRES remained active until prior to the base's closure in 1994.

Maine's Largest Daily Newspaper Yesterday's Sale 70,683

HANCOCK

Bangor Daily News

The Weather Cold

VOL. 68, NO. 179 BANGOR, MAINE, FRIDAY, JANUARY 11, 1957 TEL. 2-4881 SEVEN CENTS

Report Pilot Flying Partly Hooded

SIX DIE IN FLAMING BOMBER CRASH

Muskie Asks Added $16 Million

$82¼ Million Budget Proposed For State

By EARL ARONSON

AUGUSTA, Jan. 10 (AP)—A record balanced budget of 82¼ million dollars and a supplemental budget of nearly 16 million—the latter to be financed by a sales tax boost—were proposed for Maine today by Democratic Gov. Edmund S. Muskie.

Governor Has Budget Problem, Too-- Baby Girl

SOME OPPOSE TAX

Loring Jet Explodes Near Canada Border

Hooded For Test

WASHINGTON, Jan. 10 (AP)—A huge B52 jet bomber, its pilot partly hooded to test his reflexes, crashed in Canada today with the loss of six lives.

Search Hampered

ANDOVER, N. B., Jan. 10—Darkness and a heavy snow cover tonight hampered a search for two missing members of the crew of a Loring Air Force Base B52 bomber which exploded and crashed earlier in the day, killing six men.

20 MILES FROM BASE

SURVIVOR LISTED

(Staff Photo By Barrows)

First Blood from the Maine Skies: Inevitably, aircraft accidents occur during operations. Loring's first B-52 accident occurred on January 10, 1957, when B-52D (s/n 55-0082) crashed 10 miles from the base runway. The crew of 55-0082 was: Captain Richard A Jenkins (aircraft commander); Captain William C Davidson; Captain John E McCune; Captain Marquid H.D. Myers; Lieutenant Anders P. Larson; Lieutenant Walter A Thomas, Jr.; First Lieutenant Charles Cole; and Technical Sergeant Ray Miller (gunner). One crewman parachuted to safety and survived: Lt. Joe L. Church. On July 29, 1958, B-52D (s/n 55-0093) crashed 3 miles south of Loring AFB, killing eight of nine occupants: Major Kirkwood C. Myers (aircraft commander); Lt Lane L. Kittle (pilot); Major Milo C. Johnson (radar navigator); Lt Leonard M. Corsaro (radar navigator); Master Sergeant Oran C. Riley (gunner); 2Lt Leslie N. Martin, Jr. (navigator); 1Lt Robert E. Testerman (ECM instructor); and 2Lt James E. Thompson (ECM operator). The lone survivor was Major Moody E. Deaton (instructor pilot).

Maine's Largest Daily Newspaper Yesterday's Sale 75,087

Bangor Daily News

The Weather Sunny

VOL. 70, NO. 37 CITY BANGOR, MAINE, WEDNESDAY, JULY 30, 1958 TEL. 2-4881 SEVEN CENTS

Eight Perish As Loring B-52 Explodes

Lebanon Crisis To Continue

One Man Survives Limestone Blast; Buildings Shaken

LIMESTONE, July 29—Eight men died when a giant B-52 jet bomber exploded in a grain field here this morning.

Air Force officials said there was one survivor, Major Moody E. Deaton of Denison, Texas, an instructor pilot for the 75th Bomb Squadron at Loring Air Force.

Panel Says Hale Winner Of Election

CHARRED REMAINS—A charred scrap heap is all that remains of a once mighty bomber, a B-52 stationed at Loring AFB that crashed and burned Tuesday morning killing eight crew members. The plane crashed in a grain field about two miles from the base. A board of inquiry is investigating the cause of the fiery tragedy. (Staff Photo by Vosear).

SURVIVOR COMFORTED—The lone survivor, Maj. Moody E. Deaton of Denison, Tex., lower right, is comforted by an air corpsman at the scene of the crash. (AP Photofax).

Fair

Minneapolis Morning Tribune

Vol. XCII—No. 116 MINNEAPOLIS, MINN., WEDNESDAY, SEPTEMBER 17, 1958

7 Fliers Killed as Blazing Jet Bomber Crashes

EYEWITNESS ACCOUNTS

Family Escapes With Lives, But Loses Everything

The Kahls lost everything but their lives.

"By a miracle," they said later, the flaming jet bomber that crashed in the yard of their Inver township farm home Tuesday did not kill them all.

"Everything, everything else is gone, even the three cows," said August Kahl.

At 8:17 p.m. six Kahls were inside their farm home. The grandfather, Edward, 81, was in his bed upstairs.

In the kitchen downstairs were the mother, Anna, 42; daughters, Corene, 17; Ruth Ann, 12; Emogene, 14, and Lynn Susan, 5.

All Dive Under Table

"We were all in the kitchen, except grandfather," Corene said. "We were sitting at the table getting ready to study. Mother was standing. So was Lynn Susan.

"All of a sudden we heard this high-pitched whine like a jet but louder. It was a terrible screaming sound.

"Mother yelled, 'Get under the table.' I guess this is what saved us because we all dove under the table and the glass and stuff flew all over the house."

The wall was caved in by the explosion, the youngster said. And grandfather, confused by the incident, came downstairs and then started back up again.

"Daddy had to go after him and take him out," Ruth Ann said.

Kahl, 51, and son Loren, 15, were standing in the doorway of their barn some 30 yards from the house. They had just finished loading their pickup truck with red tomatoes picked that afternoon.

"It was like a big meteor," said Kahl later, his face swathed in bandages.

"It was like a ball of fire," said Loren.

"It was coming right at me," Loren said. "Daddy said 'let's get out of here' and started to run.

"I turned my back but before I could get going I was knocked flat on the ground.

"There was terrible heat and the barn was on fire."

Mrs. Kahl ordered the girls out of the house.

"Glass and plaster started flying all around. I told the kids to get underneath the table. More glass and

Family
Continued on Page Eight

Two Pages of Pictures From Crash Scene--Pages 12 and 13

Crowds gathered quickly at the August Kahl farm when air force B52 jet crashed, killing seven

11 Injured in Crash Near City

Farmhouse, Two Barns Burn After Plane Explodes

Seven crewmen were killed Tuesday when a blazing air force B52 jet bomber crashed on a Dakota county farm in Inver township at 8:17 p.m.

The crash occurred on the August Kahl farm about two miles south of Hwy. 218, just east of Hwy. 55.

The Kahls were routed out of their house when the giant eight-engine bomber plowed a 300-foot furrow in a field and dug a 15-foot-deep crater about 125 yards from the house.

The family was sprayed with burning jet fuel.

EIGHT members of the Kahl family and a neighbor child were taken to Riverview hospital, West St. Paul. They are:

August Kahl, 51, second and third degree burns of face and hands. Condition fair.

Loren Kahl, 15, second and third degree burns of face and hands. Condition fair.

Edward Kahl, 81, father of August, head cuts and burns on both feet. Condition good.

Corene Kahl, 17, foot cut and burned hand. She was treated and released.

Lynn Kahl, 5, burned arm. Treated and released.

Mrs. Anna Kahl, 42, August's wife, burns of both hands and ear cut. Treated

THE PRICE OF ETERNAL VIGILANCE: On September 16, 1958, B-52D (s/n 55-0065) was on a routine training mission over Minnesota when the aircraft rapidly descended at high speed after losing the vertical stabilizer, before crashing into a farmhouse near Inver Grove Heights (MN) approximately 7.5 miles south of Saint Paul (MN). The crew of 55-0065 was: Captain William C. Horstman (aircraft commander); Captain Richard J. Cantwell (navigator); Major Surles. O. Gillespie, Jr. (radar navigator); First Lieutenant William F. Huskey (ECM operator); Technical Sergeant Leon R. Lew (tail gunner); Captain James D. Taylor (radar navigator instructor); and Captain Bernard D. Lanois (instructor). The lone survivor of the crash was Captain Jack D. Craft (co-pilot). On September 4, 1969, B-52G (s/n 58-0215) crashed immediately after takeoff from Loring AFB during an ORI. The crew of 58-0215 (from lower left corner, clockwise): Major Robert M. Murray (ECM operator); Major Nils Oxehufwud (aircraft commander); Captain Theodore A. Burbank (navigator); Master Sergeant Earl J. Barnes (gunner); Lieutenant Colonel Robert C. Smith (radar navigator); and Captain William N. Payne (co-pilot). Not pictured is Colonel Homer C. Bell, Jr. (observer/ORI inspector).

GROUND LOSSES AT LORING: Of the six recorded losses of B-52s at Loring, these two were caused by ground accidents that enveloped the two large bombers. Above, B-52D (s/n 55-0102) lifts its nose skyward as it melts by fire. Below, Loring firefighters fight the blaze enveloping B-52G (s/n 58-0208). In today's parlance, both losses would be categorized as an "Aviation Class A Mishap," resulting in direct cost totaling $2 million or more, fatality or permanent total disability, or destruction of a DoD aircraft. What the events were categorized in their time is unknown, but the impact to the U.S. strategic deterrent was measurable: the unintended removal of two nuclear-capable bombers from the alert force.

INTERCEPTORS ON THE NORTHERN EDGE: Loring's location at high northern latitudes was a boon to U.S. war planners for both the offensive actions of the B-36 and B-52 fleets (and their KC-97/KC-135 tankers), and for defensive actions via interceptor aircraft against enemy bombers. Loring was home to three squadrons of Air Defense Command fighter interceptor squadrons (27 FIS, 83 FIS, 49 FIS) over its history. Staff Sergeant Larry Stafford, a jet engine technician with the 83 FIS, stands next to "his" F-106, *c.* the early 1970s. The 83 FIS replaced the 27 FIS (the patch above Stafford's nametape) in July 1971 until its inactivation in June 1972. Two F-106s (left unknown serial, right is 59-0024) belonging to the 49 FIS, Detachment 1, sit in an alert hangar at Loring. During the 1980s, the detachment helped support training as aggressors during a local exercise series dubbed "Potato Flag," in honor of Maine's crop of spuds and the Air Force's "Red Flag" exercises. (*Top photo courtesy of Ashley Copley*)

LORING'S CONTRIBUTION TO SPACE RECONNAISSANCE: During the early days of the Space Race, the Central Intelligence Agency began launching a series of film-based photographic reconnaissance satellites (1959–1972) to image the Soviet Union over the USSR. This satellite program—designated Corona—had a glaring meteorological weakness: cloud-cover. With parts of the Soviet Union shrouded by clouds 85 percent of the time, Corona planners needed a way to photograph around the cloud cover. Enter the Defense Meteorological Satellite Program (DMSP), a weather satellite used for the National Reconnaissance Program's photographic planning efforts. Without these DMSP weather forecasts, roughly 38–40 percent of the imagery returned would have been cloud-free. The first cadre arrived at Loring AFB's Blotner Radar Site in June 1963 for facility and system installation to command and downlink DMSP data. The DMSP Block 5D-2 pictured contained a variety of sensors for meteorological remote sensing, including the operational line scan system (OLS). The OLS' visible and infrared sensors collect images globally across a 3,000-km swath, twice per day, enabling the construction of an image showing lights on Earth during nighttime.

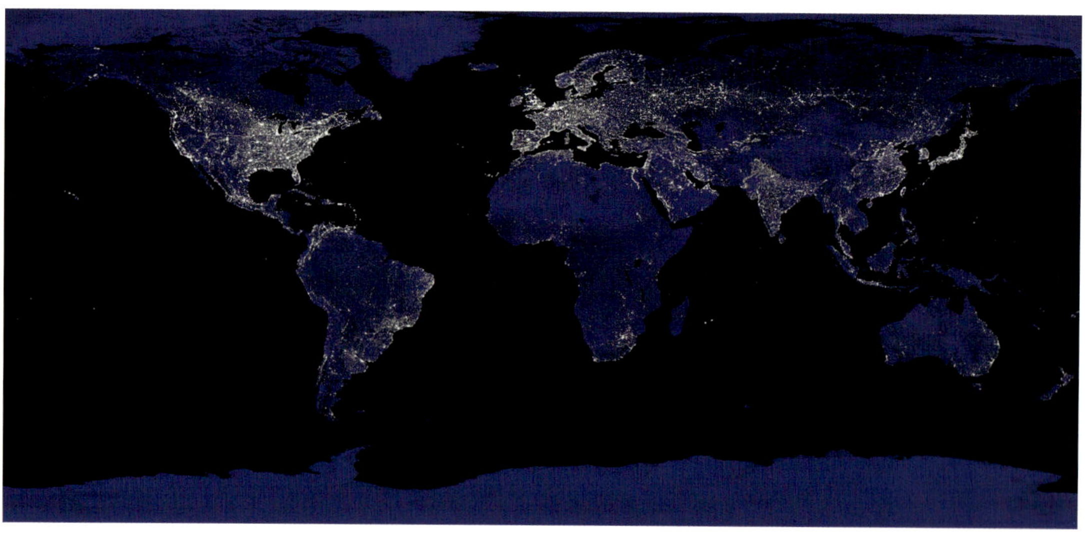

"Four Grand" Becomes the First All-Blue Suit Space Unit in the U.S. Military:

On July 10, 1963, Detachment 2, 4000th Support Group claimed initial satellite contacts with the first ever "Blue Suit" (all military) space operation in the USAF. The large white radomes protected sensitive electronic equipment from Maine's extreme climate. During the Vietnam War, DMSP data was used to plan aircraft strikes against the North Vietnamese. The mission increased during the Gulf War, through the blinding sands of the Middle Eastern deserts. DMSP information was routed to Global Weather Central headquarters at Offutt AFB (NE), being later pushed out to global SAC forces (among many other customers)—such as the Loring B-52 crews—for mission planning. Over the decades, DMSP underpinned the operations of the U.S. military, commanding the satellites and downlinking data from two coastal locations: Loring (ME) and Fairchild AFB (WA).

DELIVERER OF THE "DECLARATION OF CONSCIENCE" AGAINST MCCARTHYISM AND IDAHO POTATOES: Senator Margaret Chase Smith (ME-R) (1897–1995) expertly championed causes that represented her Maine constituents. During one episode during the late 1950s, a congressional complaint to Smith's office alleged that a sack of Idaho potatoes was found at the Loring chow (dining) hall. The subsequent investigation did not substantiate the claim, but fact finders identified that during 1958 the U.S. Army purchased over $1.1 million ($11.5 million in 2023) worth of Maine potatoes for the military services. Smith was commissioned as a lieutenant colonel in the Air Force Reserves (1950–1958) and became the first woman in Congress to break the sound barrier aboard an F-100 Super Sabre on December 3, 1957. Here she is seen visiting Loring in the mid-1950s with Secretary of the Air Force Harold Talbott (left, in the hat) and Brigadier General Bertram Harrison during a subsequent trip in January 1964.

5

Famous Faces at Loring

On December 13, 1957, Loring was host to President Dwight Eisenhower during a brief stopover before a transatlantic flight aboard *Columbine III* for the 1957 Paris summit, bringing together the leaders from the North Atlantic Treaty Organization (NATO) member nations together for the first time. Local newspapers reported that President Eisenhower "turned down" Maine delicacies from the non-commissioned officers' (NCO) club such as boiled lobster, baked potatoes, clam chowder, and green beans in exchange for roast beef, tomato juice, and shrimp cocktail. Eisenhower had suffered a stroke three weeks prior and had a healthier diet imposed by his physicians.

TRICKY DICK COMES TO MAINE: Some 5,000 Mainers came to greet President Richard Nixon and First Lady Pat Nixon on July 3, 1974, during a refueling stop at Loring. Base personnel prepared the installation by mowing lawns, spraying for insects, "policing" cigarette butts, and even flying in special stairs for deplaning from Air Force One. Nixon was welcomed home by Vice President Gerald R. Ford after lengthy arms control talks with the Soviet Union. First Lady Pat Nixon (far left), daughter Mrs. Julie Eisenhower (left center), and Vice President Ford (center-left of Nixon) watch as the president gives a speech inside the DC hangar.

VIKINGS AND VIPS: Members of the Caribou High School Band pose with their plumed hats and maroon jackets, preparing to greet President Richard Nixon on his arrival at Loring on July 3, 1974. According to Former Caribou HS Band Director Kenneth Matthews, immediately after Nixon stepped off the egress staircase from Air Force One, he walked over to meet the band members. On October 19, 1978, First Lady Rosalynn Carter arrived at Loring AFB to promote the campaign of Senator William D. Hathaway (ME-D). First Lady Carter visited Madawaska High School to meet locals, then departed in the evening for Bangor.

GROUNDBREAKING WITH MAINE'S SENATORS:
Representative Olympia J. Snowe (ME-R), second from the left, and Senator William S. Cohen (ME-R), second from the right, and other dignitaries break ground for a new base hospital on November 8, 1985. The $300 million hospital project helped bolster any attacks on Loring's closure, after what nearly occurred in the late-1970s. Senator Snowe stated the new hospital facility "was long overdue." Due to an earthquake in 1982, the medical group was restricted to using one wing inside the weakened building structure. Senator Cohen would later serve as secretary of defense (1997–2001) under President William J. Clinton.

6

New Era of Strategic Deterrence

The creation of the AGM-69A SRAM brought new nuclear-tipped "teeth" to the strategic bomber fleet. Realizing the Soviet Union possessed a formidable air defense system, SAC required a way to penetrate the airspace without incurring unacceptable losses in equipment and personnel. While the AGM-28 Hound Dog provided a stand-off solution, the two missiles were too heavy, limiting the ability of the B-52 to accomplish its strategic attack mission. Specific Hound Dog-armed B-52s would "clear" air defenses, while other Stratofortresses struck strategic targets. The replacement missile—SRAM—was significantly smaller and more lethal, allowing G- and H-models of the B-52 to carry twenty SRAMs (eight on an internal rotary launcher, six on each wing), along with their other weapons. The SRAM program was initiated on November 23, 1963, with missiles delivered to its first operational customer—the 42d Bomb Wing—in early 1972.

THE WHITE FINGERS OF DEATH: SRAM missiles sit on two pylons aboard a B-52G on Loring's ramp. Of note, this image was taken between late 1972 and 1976, due to the missing "jowls" of the AN/ASQ-151 electro-optical viewing system (EVS). The EVS system provided low-light and infrared cameras for aircrews to fly by and was installed fleetwide on B-52Gs and B-52Hs between 1971 and 1976. An up-close image of the AGM-69A SRAM at the Defense Nuclear Weapons School (DNWS) belies the missile's most notable feature: its surface "skin." Colloquially known by aircrews as the "Nerf missile," after the popular line of soft toys and projectiles, the SRAM's outer surface was covered by a special heat-protective rubber-like ablative-type material about 0.7 inches thick. This rubbery covering enabled thermal dissipation from the projectile's high speeds and absorbed incoming electromagnetic energy, lowering the missile's visibility to enemy radar operators. (*Missile photo courtesy of the author*)

FIRST LAUNCH OF A SRAM BY A SAC COMBAT CREW: On March 4, 1972, the first operational AGM-69A SRAM was delivered to Loring, and the first live five of the SRAM by a SAC Combat Crew took place over White Sands Missile Range (NM) on June 15, 1972. The Loring aircrew included Captain Ehrie (aircraft commander); Captain Rand (co-pilot); Captain Dermody, Jr (radar navigator); Captain Moran (navigator); Captain Barroquiero (EWO); and TSgt Schryer (gunner). Between September 1972 and July 1973, 42d Bomb Wing aircrews and aircraft conducted an extensive operational evaluation and testing program on the SRAM weapon system, flying a total of fifty-six captive and seventeen live-launch flights.

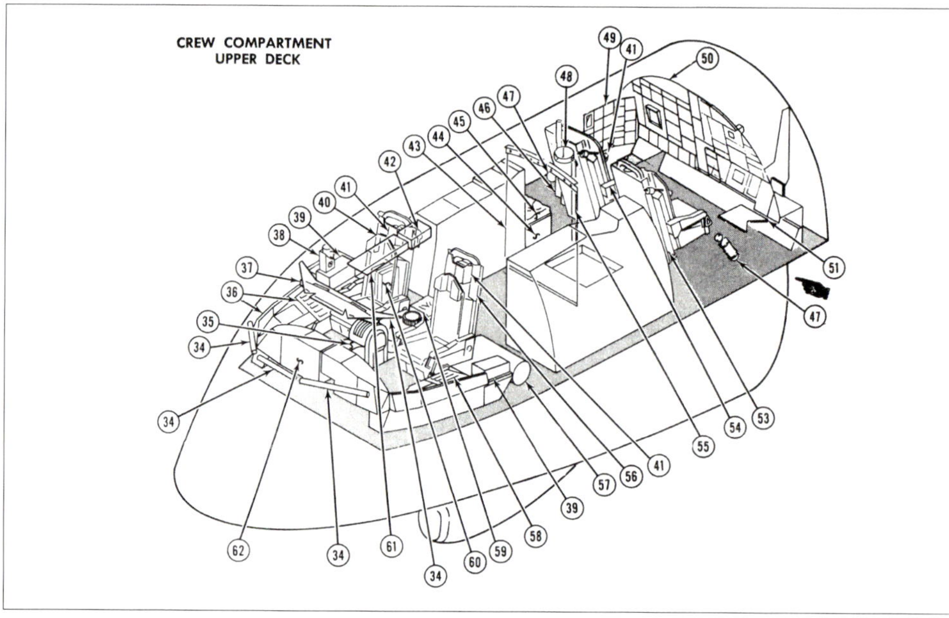

CREW POSITIONS WITHIN THE STRATOFORTRESS, PART 1: This illustration from the B-52G technical order, colloquially known as a "Dash One," shows the crew positions on the upper deck. Facing toward the nose, on the top left side is the aircraft commander—here seen as 69 BS Captain Starling—sometimes known as the pilot. Opposite the pilot on the top right side of the crew compartment (not shown) is the co-pilot. While their stations have differences in switches, knobs, and dials, many critical functions—such as the engine throttles—are located between the two for easy access by either crewmember.

Crew Positions within the Stratofortress, Part 2: The rear-facing seats on the upper deck held the electronic warfare officer (EWO, or "E-dub") on the aircraft's port (left) side, and the aerial gunner on the aircraft's starboard (right) side (in the photo, however, the gunner is on the left and EWO on the right). In command of a suite of defensive electronic equipment, the EWO ensured the aircraft survived to strike the designated targets and then egress the area. The aerial gunner position was moved from the tail into the main cabin in the B-52 G- and H-versions, allowing for better crew coordination (and an ejection seat). The radar navigator (right) had primary responsibility for the aircraft's offensive weapons, including the "special" (thermonuclear) weapons.

MAINTENANCE, 42D BOMB WING STYLE: Senior Airman Mike Pacheco and Airman Robert Morrision de-ice the tail of a KC-135 Stratotanker aircraft at Loring in late 1984, spraying warmed-up de-icing fluid from an elevated ladder and hose. Aircraft icing is a deadly hazard in cold climates, and a routine problem in Northern Tier locations such as Loring. When ice collects on wings and control surfaces, it hampers their function and may change the aircraft's lift properties. Additionally, windscreens/canopies, radio antennas, pilot tubes, and static vents/carburetors/air intakes may get clogged with ice, preventing proper function. Finally, the additional weight of the ice may strain the airframe and thrust ability of the engines, causing a crash. Three 42d Munitions Maintenance Squadron (42 MMS) airmen service an AGM-69A SRAM at position #2 on the rotary launcher within in the bomb bay of a B-52G. The technical complexity of the SRAM as seen by the diagnostic equipment and cable connectors, and the work required to maintain it as an effective deterrent belies the simplicity of the concept: nuke air defenses as the B-52 flies toward its target.

ALL JOBS ARE VITAL ON SAC'S PREMIER SUPERBASE: An unidentified airman first class (A1C) works on a radar scope within the Air Traffic Control tower at Loring in late 1986. Military ATC towers work in conjunction with FAA Air Route Traffic Control Centers (ARTCCs), such as Boston Center, to help route civil and military aircraft through their portion of the National Airspace System (NAS). Repair work like this is critical to both military mission success and safety of civilian life passing in the skies above. Airman First Class (A1C) Bushey holds an approximately 8-inch-long lag bolt in his left hand, presumably found after a foreign object debris (FOD) walk on the Loring ramp. Items smaller than a pebble and as large as the lag bolt (or larger) cause extreme to catastrophic damage to jet engines during run-up for flight or during maintenance. During a FOD walk, airmen line up evenly across the width of the ramp on one end then walk to a predetermined stopping point, searching for pieces of foreign debris as they walk down the flightline.

WAITING FOR THE KLAXON, PART 1: Chariots of the Tanker TOADs sit on Loring's parking ramp in the early 1980s during an ORI. KC-135As (serials 59-1507; 56-3624; 58-0030; 63-7977; and 57-1469) await their crews and the Emergency War Order (EWO) message to begin minimal interval take-off (MITO) to get airborne. The acronym TOAD illustrated the bleakness of the aerial tanker crew's task: "Take Off and Die," as their primary mission was to get airborne and refuel bombers heading over the North Pole toward their targets. Whether they had enough fuel to land or a recovery base to return to was immaterial to SAC planners. KC-135A Stratotankers start their maximum sortie surge—also known as an "elephant walk"—with Stratofortresses (extreme upper left) during an early 1980s ORI.

WAITING FOR THE KLAXON, PART 2: A reverse angle shot of the mixture of 42d Bomb Wing KC-135A Stratotankers and B-52G Stratofortresses during an ORI "elephant walk." Maximum sortie generation was the planned goal during ORIs but was considered unachievable with practicality if a "bolt out of the blue" struck Loring. The Emergency War Order (EWO) message received by the Command Post forced a klaxon alert, with alert crews running toward their aircraft for rapid takeoff before incoming nuclear warheads detonated on or over Loring AFB. Once airborne, B-52G aircrews would look for a friendly tanker, such as this KC-135A, from their home base or another location if the tankers got airborne in time. In the early 1980s, SAC planners were worried about tankers over Europe being shot down while in support of NATO, prompting the dark grey green "Shamu" (after the popular SeaWorld Orca attraction) scheme seen here. The scheme was only partially effective, hiding the Stratotanker when viewed from above over cloudless terrain, but making it more visible in the air.

LORING STRATOTANKERS CREATE THE AIR BRIDGE TO EUROPE: A refueling specialist connects a fuel transfer hose to a refueling truck at Loring in the mid-1980s. While otherwise important for any U.S. Air Force flying base, refueling capacity was critical to SAC bases that maintained tanker task forces, large *ad hoc* task-focused groups with large numbers of aerial tankers assigned. 42 ARS and 407 ARS aircraft were assigned to the Loring Tanker Task Force throughout the 1970s assisting with Crested Cap and other Tactical Air Command fighter deployments to Europe, as well as the European Tanker Task Force. By providing Air Refueling Control Points (ARCPs) over the mid-Atlantic, Loring-based aircrews helped drag the fighters toward Europe or back towards North America on their return adventures. Here, KC-135A (s/n 61-0325) assigned to the 42d Bomb Wing rests at RAF Mildenhall after a European Tanker Task Force support mission in September 1986. (*KC-135 image courtesy of Rob Schleiffert via Creative Commons*)

DOUBLING UP LORING'S AERIAL FUELING CAPACITY: Loring doubled its refueling ability in July 1968 with the addition of the 407th Air Refueling Squadron (407 ARS). The unit's cattle motif logo originates from its early days at Malmstrom AFB (MT) as a KB-29P and later KC-97, air refueling squadron. After supporting Cuban Missile Crisis flying operations in 1962 from Homestead AFB (FL) with the 19th Bombardment Wing, the 407 ARS eventually moved to Loring later in the decade. As part of the East Coast Tanker Task Force, Loring units helped support the development of the B-1B bomber project in the early 1980s. The B-1 was revived by President Ronald Reagan in 1981 after being cancelled by President Jimmy Carter in June 1977. This aircraft is B-1A (s/n 76-0174) in European One camouflage being refueled by a Loring tanker in the early 1980s. Used as an avionics test bed, this B-1A is closer in evolution to the B-1B follow-on with ejection seats (instead of an ejecting crew compartment) and other advanced features. The visible dorsal spine is a feature unique to the B-1A variants. The Loring refueling mission came during the B-1A's "East Coast tour," departing Eglin AFB's McKinley Climatic Chamber for realistic testing with the Northern Tier cold weather temperatures.

AirSea Battle Comes to Fruition, Part 1: During the rise of Soviet naval power in the 1970s and 1980s, U.S. military war planners created a symbiotic relationship—called AirSea Battle doctrine—between the U.S. Air Force and U.S. Navy, with aircrews providing maritime surveillance (in the Busy Observer program) and anti-ship strike capability with newly developed AGM-84 Harpoon anti-ship missile. In 1983, Loring-based B-52Gs were modified to carry the 100-mile range Harpoon missiles. A Loring-based B-52G flies into position to fire an AGM-84 Harpoon missile at a target hulk during Harpoonex, a phase of Fleet Exercise (FLEETEX) 2-86 on April 20, 1986. A missile training round, designated ATM-84C, is seen hanging off a B-52G pylon as aircrew and maintainers discuss mission particulars during a training exercise. Most American military ordnance have training variants to allow sufficiently realistic simulation of loading and unloading or even live fire (with no warhead detonation) prior to combat usage.

AIRSEA BATTLE COMES TO FRUITION, PART 2: Another boon to Loring's AirSea Battle capabilities was the addition of the Mark 60 CAPTOR (encapsulated torpedo) anti-submarine naval mine. Issuance to the 42d Bomb Wing was not an accident, for U.S. planners wanted to provide a way to create a lower cost barrier minefield across the GIUK (Greenland–Iceland–United Kingdom) Gap known to contain transiting Soviet submarines and surface traffic heading toward North America. An aluminum shell anchored to the ocean floor contained a Mark 46 homing torpedo with an underwater lifespan of weeks to months. Sound propagation electronics allowed the CAPTOR mine to passively identify traffic and distinguish between hostile submarines and surface vessels and friendly submarines. A B-52G ejects a lone CAPTOR mine via parachute over the Atlantic during test trials in the mid-1980s.

Competitive Spirit Helps Loring Go Out On-Top: SAC's Bombing and Navigation Competition took many names over the years. From 1971 through 1987, it would be known as Giant Voice. Just like the crews put forth decades earlier, the 42d Bomb Wing identified their best crews to compete against the other SAC bombardment and air refueling wings. The base photo lab created this photo montage for Giant Voice 1980, comprising of wing leadership, along with Loring's competitors: Bomber Crews R-19 and S-02, and Tanker Crews E122 and S101. During the 34th Annual Bombing and Navigation Competition (renamed Proud Shield) the 42d Bomb Wing won the William J. Crumm Linebacker Memorial Trophy for the "Best B-52 crew in high altitude bombing," held by celebrating crew members. The trophy is named for Maj.-Gen. William J. Crumm, former commander of the 3d Air Division, who died on a combat mission in 1967 when his B-52 crashed into the South China Sea. The trophy was donated by Boeing Aerospace Corporation in memory of the B-52 crews killed in Operation Linebacker II over North Vietnam. This Proud Shield competition was held April 13–15, 1992, and was the last one held by SAC, which was inactivated on June 1, 1992.

LORING'S MILITARY WORKING DOGS: The U.S. military uses military working dogs in all branches. The dogs are trained for specific jobs to include human tracking, explosive detection, patrol, search and rescue, and attack. Loring's security specialists took time to carefully train the dogs to perform tasks, showing off their dogs' capabilities during public events like airshows or other community engagements. So beloved by their handlers were Loring's military working dogs, a special cemetery was created when they died. While the 42d Combat Defense Squadron Sentry Dog Cemetery has fallen into disrepair over the decades, there are ongoing efforts to preserve the memory and memories to these four-legged warriors.

THE MOOSE PLANS FOR THE NEXT FLYING MISSION FROM MAINE: An angry moose motif adorns the tail of a 42d Bomb Wing B-52G (s/n 58-0202) while participating in an exercise in Hawaii. Loring's moose has been a central part of many logos on 42d Bomb Wing aircraft, both bombers and tankers, appearing as silhouettes, on 42 ARS tankers, or as a caricature on a Stratofortress fin as seen here. Captain Mike Pompoco, far right, briefs a 69th Bomb Squadron aircrew during Ghost Warrior, a joint air force/navy exercise conducted during late November 1989. Mission planning is a team event, requiring input from all members of an aircrew, allowing experience and training to help guide decision making required during a flying mission. The aircrew members are (from left): Staff Sergeant Clint Coleman, First Lieutenant Jim Turner, Captain Gary Maynard, Captain James Faber, and Captain Rich Stuckey.

PLAYING WAR GAMES IN THE GREAT NORTH: An unidentified U.S. Navy captain supporting Ghost Warrior is greeted upon arrival at Loring by two 42d Bomb Wing colonels on November 1, 1989. Ghost Warrior was joint exercise conducted during the base's conventional ORI, allowing evaluation of the wing's ability to execute parts of the AirSea Battle doctrine, such as laying CAPTOR mines or conducting anti-ship operations with the AGM-84 Harpoon missile. Other practice engagements included local exercises such as North Moose 93-2, a simulated deployment for practicing air base ground defense tactics. Two 42d security policemen wear chemical warfare defense equipment, arctic camouflage, and multiple integrated laser engagement system (MILES) gear on their helmets and M-16 rifles.

Closing the Cold War's Final Chapter: Munition maintainers load a clip of four Mark 28 thermonuclear bombs inside a B-52G. These four gravity bombs, along with a load of AGM-69A SRAMs provided enough firepower to destroy any enemy air defenses and primary targets within the Soviet Union. As the Cold War came to a close during the final years of the 1980s, Pentagon war planners reoriented many B-52G units into conventional roles, including the 42d Bomb Wing. On October 1, 1988, the front page of the *Bangor Daily News* ran an article titled "Loring bombers end nuclear for first time since October 1957." Five enthusiastic aircrew members celebrate the significance (and signage) of "No Alert" inside the Alert Facility. The next challenge for these aircrew members was just around the corner, appearing in the Middle Eastern desert during the summer of 1990.

THE NEXT GENERATION OF WARFARE: On August 2, 1990, the Iraqi Army invaded the sovereign State of Kuwait. Within six days of the invasion, the first American aircraft—F-15s from the 1st Tactical Fighter Wing—arrived in Saudi Arabia for combat air patrols. The continuous shipment of aircraft, personnel, and materiel to the Middle East saw Loring as a prime stop-over location. KC-135 and KC-10 tankers provided air-refueling for aircrews heading to European bases, while also enabling a large cargo delivery capacity. Here a KC-10 Extender is loaded via the side door during a stop at Loring AFB on February 22, 1991.

THE TWILIGHT WAR OF THE G-MODEL STRATOFORTRESSES: Prior to the kickoff of Operation Desert Storm, B-52Gs from the 42d Bomb Wing helped outfit provisional bomb wings at Moron air base, Spain (801st); Jeddah, Saudi Arabia (1708th); and Diego Garcia, British Indian Ocean Territory (4300th). The aircraft held colorful names such as *East Coast Outlaw*, *Eternal Guardian*, and *Thunder Struck*. Accompanying artwork was painted over and hidden while deployed but was repainted when the aircraft returned to Loring. The 4300th Bomb Wing (Provisional) morale patch states "Fire from the Island," as the fire-breathing dragon holds a bomb in one talon and an air-refueling boom in the other.

COMACC Visits Loring: During a September 1992 visit to Loring, commander of Air Combat Command (COMACC), Gen. John M. Loh holds aloft a thank you plaque from the men and women of the 42d Bomb Wing. As the commander of Tactical Air Command (TAC), General Loh became the first commander of Air Combat Command (ACC) upon its creation and subsequent disestablishment of TAC and SAC on June 1, 1992. The creation of ACC from the ashes of SAC and TAC attempted to establish a new paradigm that made Operation Desert Storm successful—the merging of aircraft and capabilities to achieve objectives based on mission, not whether an asset is labeled "tactical" versus "strategic." This paradigm would last until 2009, when Air Force Global Strike Command stood up to corral the disintegrating nuclear enterprise.

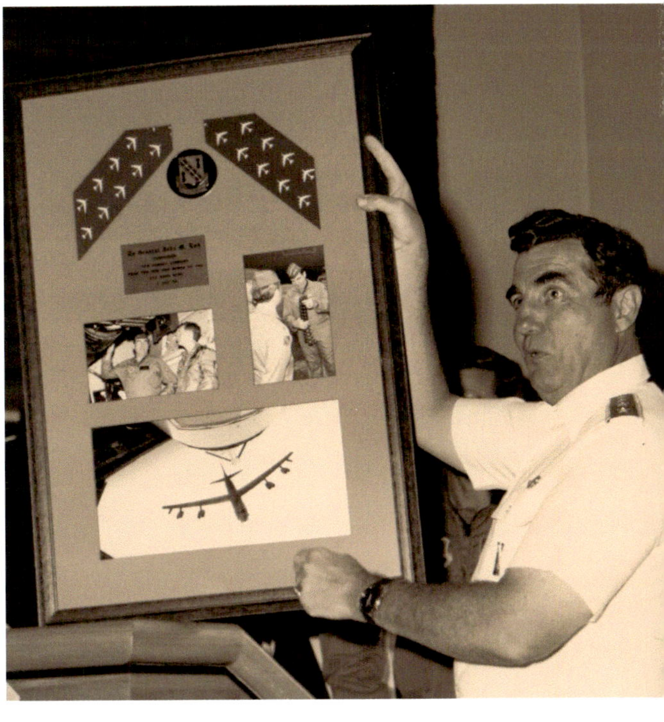

A Final Farewell to the Citizens of "The County": While the BRAC decision shook the reality of the communities of Caribou and Limestone, the resident air force members had to plan and execute a major transition from active military air base to former defense facility status after the departure of flying operations in late 1993. Above, the sign that stood the test of time, recognizing the friendship between military and civilian communities was adorned one last time with "Thank you Aroostook."

7

Loring's Legacy

During the 1983 thriller *WarGames*, the protagonist hacker tricks a wargaming supercomputer with artificial intelligence to "play" a game of Global Thermonuclear War. Unable to distinguish between electronic-generated fantasy and reality, U.S. military members decide to counterattack their adversary using SAC's nuclear alert force, only waiting until the last minute to ride out the initial wave of incoming Soviet missiles. Loring Air Force Base is identified as one of the first targets to be destroyed, though the 42d Bomb Wing was misidentified as the "43d Bomb Wing." Brave (fictional) Airman Dougherty answered the call from the NORAD commander since the Senior Command Post controller was away from his station.

GHOSTS OF LORING, PART 1: Inside view of the arch hangar from September 1998 shows how well it has held up since the base closing in 1994. Note at the far left of the image, the words stating, "42 FMS: Best in the Air Force 1989." The nondescript close-up shot of the Alert Area apron, better known as the "Crows Feet" or "Christmas Tree," downplays the enormous destructive power that sat here patiently over nearly three decades. (*Courtesy of the National Park Service/HAER ME-64*)

GHOSTS OF LORING, PART 2: The most distinctive feature of the crew readiness building was the number of tunnels projecting from the basement and ground levels to give aircrews clear access to their aircraft on the alert apron once the alert klaxon sounded. The building received the nickname "The Mole Hole," due to these numerous corrugated steel tunnels throughout. The double cantilever (DC) hangar sits among the rest of Loring's ruins, waiting for new occupants or returnees to help tell its story. (*Courtesy of the National Park Service/HAER ME-64*)

FINAL FORMATION OF BUFFS: A collection of B-52G Stratofortresses await their final fate at Davis-Monthan AFB (AZ) during July 1996. The G-model accounted for 26 percent of B-52s produced (193 of the total 744), the most numerous variant. After signature of the Strategic Arms Reduction Treaty (START) on July 31, 1991, each nuclear-capable B-52 in storage at the USAF's Aircraft Maintenance and Regeneration Center (AMARC, colloquially known as the "Boneyard") was eventually guillotined into five pieces by a heavy steel blade dropped by a crane. The pieces remained visible to surveillance satellites for six months for treaty verification, before being taken to a smelter for final destruction. When USAF's Air Combat Command took control of assets after SAC's inactivation on June 1, 1992, many aircraft were given tail codes for the first time to help identify their bases of origin. Loring's B-52 bomber fleet received the tail code of "LZ." The International Air Transport Association (IATA) identifier for Loring was LIZ, while the International Civil Aviation Organization (ICAO)'s airport code was KLIZ. While not all IATA and ICAO codes match, Loring was one of the few that did. The "LZ" coded B-52Gs were awaiting destruction at Davis-Monthan AFB's AMARC, colloquially known as the "Boneyard." Many Loring "birds" were still among this collection in 1996. (*Images courtesy of Ian Abbott/Flickr.com*)

MINOT'S 5TH OPERATIONS SUPPORT SQUADRON WINS THE CHARLES J. LORING, JR. AWARD: Lt. Gen. Stephen Wilson, Air Force Global Strike Command commander presents the Maj. Charles J. Loring, Jr. Award for Best Overall Bomber Support Squadron to Col. Alexis Mezynski, 5th Bomb Wing commander, during a ceremony at Barksdale AFB (LA) on April 9, 2014. The award was presented annually to the wing recognized as the best in their field. (*U.S. Air Force photo/Senior Airman Joseph A. Pagán Jr.*)

ALTERNATIVE USES FOR A FORMER DEFENSE FACILITY: The alternative rock band Phish—"locals" from Burlington, Vermont—and their fervent fans called "Phishheads" invaded Aroostook County three times during the late 1990s and early 2000s. The festivals (The Great Went, 1997; Lemonwheel, 1998; IT, 2003) brought tens of millions of dollars back into Aroostook County. Each gathering saw over 65,000 people flock to the former Loring AFB, inadvertently creating Maine's largest "city" during the festivals' duration. No stretch of the imagination from Loring's original architects could have foreseen this, as pictured during "The Great Went," on August 15–17, 1997. The Loring Air Museum and their collection of memories and artifacts keeps the base's history alive for future generations, while allowing previous inhabitants to return and ruminate. *(Courtesy of Todd Wickersty/Flickr.com)*

Limestone Welcomes Home an Old Big Ugly Fat "Fellow": On the afternoon of August 11, 2022, a B-52 landed at the Loring Commerce Center, the first time a Stratofortress had returned since the fall of 1993. The Barksdale-based 307th Bomb Wing B-52H (s/n 60-0045) performed two flybys before popping out its 90-foot long, 200-lb drag chute when it landed on the 12,100-foot runway. The Loring Air Museum staff successfully lobbied to get the B-52 up to Maine, along with a KC-135 tanker from the 101st Air Refueling Wing, Maine Air National Guard during the reunion weekend for SAC's first superbase. An overcast day in Maine illuminates the former Loring Air Force Base's current state. *(U.S. Air Force photo/Master Sgt. Andrew Sinclair)*

THE 42D LIVES ON: The legacy of the 42d Bombardment Wing lives on as part of the 42d Air Base Wing, the host unit at Maxwell AFB (AL), and Maxwell-Gunter Annex. During Loring's closure on September 30, 1994, the 42d Bomb Wing was inactivated the same day. The inactivation was short lived, however, since the unit was re-activated and redesignated the 42d Air Base Wing the very next day. This historic continuation was part of a service-wide effort to preserve the lineage of the air force's most honored wings. (*Image courtesy of Air Force Historical Research Agency*)

About the Loring Air Museum

The Loring Air Museum is a tax-exempt organization whose mission is to tell the history of Loring Air Force Base through collections, exhibits, and educational programs. Established in 2005 as the Loring Military Heritage Center inside the former Loring Federal Credit Union, the Loring Air Museum contains permanent exhibits for the public to understand the evolution of the Limestone air base and surrounding area, educating people of all ages, and allowing former Loring military members a place to remember the past. Their address is:

Loring Air Museum
131 Cupp Road
Limestone, ME 04751
Website: loringairmuseum.com/

BIBLIOGRAPHY

Air & Space Force Association, "Namesakes: Charles Loring," *Air & Space Forces Magazine*, airandspaceforces.com/article/namesakes-charles-loring/.

Garbinski, J., *North River Depot* (Morrisville, NC: Lulu Press, 2011), books.google.com/books?id=4HXj2VV3MD8C.

Jacobsen, M., *Convair B-36: A Comprehensive History of America's 'Big Stick'* (Atglen, PA: Schiffer Military Publishing, 1997)

Kraft, V., *History of Loring Air Force Base* (Bangor, ME: Bessey and Kraft, 2000)

Maurer, M. (ed.), *Combat Squadrons of the Air Force, World War II* (Washington, DC: Office of Air Force History, 1982), media.defense.gov/2010/Dec/02/2001329899/-1/-1/0/AFD-101202-002.pdf.

National Park Service, *Historic American Engineering Record: Loring Air Force Base. HAER No. ME-64* (Philadelphia, PA: Northeast Region, Philadelphia Support Office), memory.loc.gov/master/pnp/habshaer/me/me0300/me0307/data/me0307data.pdf.

--. *Historic American Engineering Record: Loring Air Force Base, Airfield. HAER No. ME-64-A*, memory.loc.gov/master/pnp/habshaer/me/me0300/me0308/data/me0308data.pdf.

--. *Historic American Engineering Record: Loring Air Force Base, Arch Hangar. HAER No. ME-64-B*, memory.loc.gov/master/pnp/habshaer/me/me0300/me0309/data/me0309data.pdf.

--. *Historic American Engineering Record: Loring Air Force Base, Double Cantilever Hangar. HAER No. ME-64-C*, memory.loc.gov/master/pnp/habshaer/me/me0300/me0310/data/me0310data.pdf

--. *Historic American Engineering Record: Loring Air Force Base, Weapon Storage Area. HAER No. ME-64-D*, memory.loc.gov/master/pnp/habshaer/me/me0300/me0311/data/me0311data.pdf.

--. *Historic American Engineering Record: Loring Air Force Base, Alert Area. HAER No. ME-64-E*, memory.loc.gov/master/pnp/habshaer/me/me0300/me0312/data/me0312data.pdf.

Shaw, F. J. (ed.), *Locating Air Force Base Sites: History's Legacy* (Washington, D.C.: Air Force History and Museums Program, 2004), amc.af.mil/Portals/12/documents/AFD-131018-055.pdf.

War Department, 1944 Missing Air Crew Report 42-25513 (National Archives), fold3.com/image/28633388.

INDEX

About the Author

Joseph ("Joe") T. Page II is a military historian and former air force officer. The military history "bug" bit him early in life while growing up at White Sands Missile Range, New Mexico, the "Birthplace of America's Missile and Space Activity." After spending a decade in uniform, Joe and his family finally settled in Albuquerque, New Mexico. He holds degrees in English and history from the University of New Mexico. This is his third Fonthill book.